D1125940

MUSCLE SHOALS SOUND STUDIO

MUSCLE SHOALS SOUND STUDIO

HOW THE SWAMPERS CHANGED AMERICAN MUSIC

CARLA JEAN WHITLEY

THE
History
PRESS

Published by The History Press
Charleston, SC 29403
www.historypress.net

Cover design by Emily Kirby

Front cover: Copyright Tommy Wright Productions, MuscleShoalsSound.Info, SwamperTom@
icloud.com, 256-246-8106.
Back cover, top: For a time, a sign welcomed visitors to Muscle Shoals, Alabama, the hit-recording
capital of the world. *Martin Colyer*.

First published 2014
Second printing 2014

ISBN 978.1.62619.239.3

Library of Congress Cataloging-in-Publication Data

Whitley, Carla Jean.
Muscle Shoals Sound Studios : how the Swampers changed American music / Carla Jean Whitley.
pages cm
Includes bibliographical references and index.
ISBN 978-1-54020-918-4
1. Muscle Shoals Sound Studios--History. 2. Sound recording industry--Alabama--Muscle
Shoals--History. 3. Popular music--Alabama--Muscle Shoals--History and criticism. 4. Muscle
Shoals Swampers (Musical group) 5. FAME Recording Studios--History. I. Title.
ML3790.W495 2014
781.6409761'915--dc23
2014025439

For Mom and Dad, who always knew I had it in me.

CONTENTS

Foreword, by Lee Shook Jr.   9
Acknowledgements   13
Introduction: Sweet Home Alabama   15

1. The Sound of Muscle Shoals   21
2. Becoming Famous   26
3. The Swampers   32
4. The Singing River   39
5. A Slow Start   47
6. The Rolling Stones   51
7. Time to Kill   56
8. Lynyrd Skynyrd   61
9. The Staple Singers   67
10. Where Black and White Meet   72
11. The Hit Parade   76
12. Continued Success   92
13. Alabama Avenue   99
14. Noel Webster   108
15. The Black Keys   113
16. A Memorial to Music   119
17. Documenting the Sound   126
18. Marching to a New Beat   130
19. Onward   136

CONTENTS

Bibliography   143
Index   157
About the Author   159

NOW MUSCLE SHOALS HAS GOT THE SWAMPERS

When I was in high school, my father used to tell me about a keyboard-playing friend he grew up with named Barry Beckett. At the time, I had no idea who he was, other than a glowing source of pride and storytelling for my old man, who recounted all of the amazing soul records Beckett played on after leaving Birmingham's Ramsay High School in the early 1960s. Beckett worked with everyone from the Rolling Stones to Bob Dylan and Julian Lennon to Bob Seger. My father was more than effusive when talking about his old pal's musical exploits. Dad would go on and on about the first time he heard the records Beckett played on and how earth shattering they were to the kids of his generation.

I was impressed, but at the time, I was heavily into the Velvet Underground, Sonic Youth and various offshoots of grunge and psychedelia. I (foolishly) didn't take much interest in the sounds of my father's youth.

But as I grew older and my record collection began to expand in ever-increasing leaps and bounds in college, I kept noticing Beckett's name popping up in the weirdest of places. First it was on Traffic's terrific 1973 live LP *On the Road*, where Beckett was featured alongside Steve Winwood, Jim Capaldi and the future percussionist for legendary krautrock outfit Can, Reebop Kwaku Baah. "Hmmm," I thought. "Now that's interesting."

Maybe there was more to this story than my old man was letting on.

There were also three other names on that record that I would soon realize were synonymous with high-quality LPs and an obligatory scroll through the musician credits of every album I picked up along the way.

My dad didn't know David Hood, Jimmy Johnson or Roger Hawkins—at least not personally—but he did know their music and told me about a little band they used to have up in Muscle Shoals known colloquially as "the Swampers." But wait. Wasn't there a line in Lynyrd Skynyrd's "Sweet Home Alabama" about a band called "the Swampers?" Were those the same people my dad was talking about? The ones who were "known to pick a song or two?"

At first, I was a little confused. Did my dad actually know these people? And were they the same ones who played on all of those amazing records he used to rave about? I experienced this epiphany during the pre-Internet days of the mid-'90s, and so I couldn't be sure. There wasn't yet a massive computer database to waste countless hours searching through, or Google, or Wikipedia. Instead, I had to piece together the story myself, one record at a time, as I dug ever deeper into the dusty crates and crevices of used record stores around the state of Alabama in search of a new fix.

And so it began.

Wasn't that Beckett's name on the back of Bob Dylan's *Slow Train Coming*, listed as producer? And there he was again on Paul Simon's *There Goes Rhymin' Simon* with the rest of the Swampers—just like on Dr. Hook's *Pleasure & Pain*. And was that Jimmy Johnson listed in the credits as engineer on the Rolling Stones' *Sticky Fingers*, along with a place called Muscle Shoals Sound Studio? When the hell were the Stones in Muscle Shoals recording that album anyway?

In fact, didn't Herbie Mann record an entire LP there called *Muscle Shoals Nitty Gritty* with legendary vibraphonist Roy Ayers? And weren't those all four of the Swampers playing on J.J. Cale's *Really*? Are these even the same guys? From my home state?

Little did I know that I had stumbled on one of the great cornerstones of modern music and a group of some of the finest arrangers and performers to ever come out of not just Alabama or the United States but, ultimately, the world.

These musicians hailed from a small town northwest of Birmingham, the state's largest city. The Shoals region would change the course of music history by laying the foundation for some of the most influential recordings of the twentieth century, with everyone from the Staple Singers to Delbert McClinton falling under its sway. The Muscle Shoals Rhythm Section was a cadre of brilliantly unassuming rock and soul missionaries that made its mark on history through a long list of session and production work that would rival anything coming out of Motown, Philadelphia or New York City.

The group gnashed its teeth under the hard-won tutelage of Rick Hall, from FAME Recording Studios, who not only put the group members through their paces but also helped mold them into the tireless workhorses he knew they could be. The Muscle Shoals Rhythm Section was not just a group of breakaway rebels trying to find their way in the music business with the studio at 3614 Jackson Highway but revolutionary sound sculptors who would play massive roles in almost every genre of popular music from the 1960s onward. Their work included everything: country, funk, reggae, southern rock. They could easily compete for the title of "Greatest Band You've Never Heard (But Actually Have)."

The Swampers left behind a massive catalogue of hits and (ever-so-slight) misses for crate diggers like myself to one day uncover. They sent ripples around the music industry with their mysterious backwoods pedigree and down-home charm, making their work a calling card to the world to show that Alabama—and the Shoals in particular—was among the leading lights in state-of-the-art audio craftsmanship and a place where raw sonic synergy seemed to hang in the air like the humidity on a hot summer's night by the Wilson Dam.

This is their story.

Lee Shook Jr. is a freelance writer, videographer, documentary filmmaker and concert promoter based in Birmingham, Alabama. He is also the host of the Audiovore, *a specialty radio program on Birmingham Mountain Radio that offers historical context for various strains of modern music along with in-depth interviews with artists from around the country. You can hear him at bhammountainradio.com on Sundays from 10:00 p.m. until midnight, central standard time.*

ACKNOWLEDGEMENTS

Although the act of writing a book is solitary work, this story couldn't be told without the community that has rallied around me. I firmly believe people don't thrive in isolation, and I'm so fortunate to have so many to lean on. Thanks to:

The Alternate Routes ("Nothing More") and the Lone Bellow ("Bleeding Out") for the songs I played on repeat during the final weeks of writing. You helped keep me sane and focused on the goal.

Lee Shook, whose foreword adds a personal touch.

Martin Colyer, whose images help bring this book to life.

Alabama musicians past and present, Muscle Shoals–related or not, for reminding us we have so many reasons to sing.

Charles Buchanan, whose book *Fading Ads of Birmingham* served as inspiration and who himself was always willing to offer a pep talk.

Everyone who helped edit my author bio, especially Kate Abney, Dana Jaffe and Marty Swant.

Sara Samchok, who tolerated pages and pages of notes strewn about the house for the duration of my writing process.

The Urban Standard staff, who are among my chief cheerleaders and caffeine suppliers.

Carrie Rollwagen and the entire crew at Church Street Coffee and Books, who allowed me to tell my story on the shop's blog (churchstreetshop.com) and kept me both caffeinated and inspired.

ACKNOWLEDGEMENTS

Emmet O'Neal Library for providing a quiet place to write and cheering on your patrons.

My yoga teacher, Melissa Scott, for her recurring admonition, "You are stronger than you think you are." Those words have become an uplifting mantra that resonates on and off my mat.

Co-workers past and present, from Lydia Seabol Avant, Amy Robinson and Christopher Walsh at the *Tuscaloosa News* to Paul Foreman at the *Birmingham News* to Meredith Cummings and Jennifer Greer at the University of Alabama. Your work and encouragement have reminded me why I believe in the power of journalism.

My interns and students, whom I hope have gleaned as much from my lessons as I have from being your teacher.

My compassionate, considerate colleagues at *Birmingham* magazine: Alecia Archibald, Laura Buchanan, Amy Cash, Katie Chipman, Robin Colter, Rebecca Garner, Alice Harvey, Pat Hooten, Haley Isbell, Julie Keith, David Magee, Christine Marsh, Laura McAlister, Deidra Perry, Beth Ragland, Courtney Simmons, Mary Ellen Stancill, Garrick Stone, Miles Walls and Jenny Watkins. So few people meet a new friend every time they meet a new co-worker. I'm lucky to be among you.

My college roommates Apryl Marie Fogel, Heather Lancaster Gardner, Paula Chadwick Kellam and Alison May Stuart, who always believed in me rather than thinking I was crazy (even in the moments when I probably *was* a little nutty!).

Monica Aswani, Holly Chesnut, Adam Evans, Murray Sexton Gervais, Shayne Gervais, Brad Higginbotham, Clair McLafferty, Alli Morgan and Philip Morgan—there's nothing like friends who can handle your most vulnerable and emotional moments.

The entire Whitley, Vann and Ketcham clans, who always welcome me, feed me and make me laugh.

My siblings, Cheryl Joy Miner, Chad Whitley and Cristin Whitley, who walk alongside me in pursuing a creative life.

My parents, who always hoped I'd write the great American novel. (This is nonfiction, but hey, it's a step.)

My writing buddies Mac and Harry, who were always eager to keep me company during the process.

Put Ketcham: I've always been happy with my own company, but this INFJ has found life is better at your side. I wasn't capable of understanding the phrase "other half" until I met you.

INTRODUCTION

SWEET HOME ALABAMA

Now Muscle Shoals has got the Swampers
And they've been known to pick a song or two
Lord they get me off so much
They pick me up when I'm feeling blue
Now how about you?
—*"Sweet Home Alabama," Lynyrd Skynyrd*

It isn't much to look at. In fact, passersby could be excused for overlooking the concrete block building on Jackson Highway. Who would look at that façade and guess that some of the world's most memorable music was recorded within its walls?

Muscle Shoals Sound Studio was founded in a former Gibson Blind Factory in Sheffield, Alabama, in 1969. The town itself is as unassuming as the studio's building; it's populated by fewer than ten thousand people and tucked into a far-flung corner of the state. Along with Florence, Tuscumbia and the town of Muscle Shoals—cities tucked into corners of Colbert and Lauderdale Counties—Sheffield is the heart of the Muscle Shoals Sound.

In the 1960s and '70s, the Muscle Shoals city limit sign claimed that it was the "hit recording capital of the world." That's a self-declaration no one could prove nor deny, although the number of gold and platinum records produced in these four riverside towns certainly offers strength to the claim. Muscle Shoals Sound Studio helped make the case for its truth.

W.C. Handy, widely considered the "Father of the Blues," is a Florence, Alabama native. A number of his albums appear in the Alabama Music Hall of Fame. *Author's collection.*

But in order to fully understand that building's surprising place in musical history, you've got to look at the region itself.

You go to New York, and it's Alabama, and all of these people are influenced by that river culture, or that part of the country.
—*The Staple Singers' producer Al Bell to the* Arkansas Journal, *2001*

In the 1950s, a number of black musicians were playing throughout Muscle Shoals in places such as the Elk's Club, while country and rockabilly musicians were also trying to gain traction.

But then, as now, Muscle Shoals didn't have much to offer in the way of music venues. The big difference, though, was that, at that time, no one thought you could find success recording music in Alabama.

Why? Well, partly because it hadn't been done. The state lacked music publishing companies and recording studios; Alabama musicians left the state to find success.

The legend of the now famous Muscle Shoals sound goes far beyond the region's limits. For example, the National Blues Museum is based in St. Louis, Missouri. But the "Father of the Blues" and author of the song "St. Louis Blues" is W.C. Handy, a Florence native.

That song is now an American standard and has been covered by a number of artists, including Stevie Wonder and fellow Alabamian Nat King Cole. In 2010, the *Huntsville (AL) Times* dubbed it the twelfth-best song by an

Rick Hall, founder of Florence, Alabama Music Enterprises Recording Studios. *George F. Landegger Collection of Alabama Photographs in Carol M. Highsmith's America, Library of Congress, Prints and Photographs Division. Gift, George F. Landegger, 2010 (DLC/PP-2010:090).*

Alabama artist. If such a renowned song is only ranked number twelve, it's easy to deduce that this state has produced some talent.

Fans of classic music, especially rock and rhythm and blues, will recognize a number of the songs that placed higher; Wilson Pickett's "Land of 1,000 Dances" was eleventh on that list, and Clarence Carter's "Patches" was tenth. Percy Sledge's "When a Man Loves a Woman" came in fifth. "Every time someone went to Muscle Shoals, they came out of there with a hit. You had to know there was something special in Muscle Shoals," Carter said in the 2013 documentary *Muscle Shoals.*

These songs have more in common than Alabama musicians; they were all recorded in the Shoals. Pickett and Carter both recorded at FAME (Florence Alabama Music Enterprises) Recording Studios, and Carter's "Patches" is a biographical tale written by the studio's founder Rick Hall. According to the same story in the *Huntsville Times*, the five best songs associated with Muscle Shoals Sound and its rhythm section are "Respect" by Aretha Franklin, "Brown Sugar" by the Rolling Stones, "Old Time Rock and Roll" by Bob Seger, "Kodachrome" by Paul Simon and "Sweet Soul Music" by Arthur Conley.

Back in the '60s and '70s, it was a handful of people deciding that they could do it here, that they didn't have to go to Nashville or L.A. or New York. They could do it here and still have those records heard.
—Ben Tanner, Alabama Shakes keyboardist, Single Lock Records co-owner and Muscle Shoals native, in an interview with the (University of Alabama) Crimson White, *November 4, 2013*

Although a festival now annually celebrates Handy's contributions, for decades, Alabamians had to leave the state if they wanted to record music that would get noticed. Handy (1873–1958) traveled from Birmingham to St. Louis to Memphis to New York. In the 1940s, Montgomery native Hank Williams saw some success in his home state but didn't make noise on a national scale until he performed in Nashville and found a record deal there.

The list of musicians and music industry folks who followed in their footsteps is extensive: Sam Phillips is from Florence but made music history in Memphis after he created Sun Records and recorded Elvis Presley; R&B's Dinah Washington, Nat King Cole and Lionel Richie; country music's the Louvin Brothers, Tammy Wynette and Emmylou Harris; the incomparable Sun Ra; coastal king Jimmy Buffett; members of Motown's

The cabin in which W.C. Handy was raised is now a museum and library in Florence. Handy was born in the home in 1873. He advised the city on its restoration but died before the museum opened. *Author's collection.*

Rusted metal sculptures of musicians stand outside the W.C. Handy Home, Museum and Library in Florence. The home has been designated a landmark of American music. *Author's collection.*

the Temptations. They traveled to New Orleans, Nashville, Memphis and as far afield as Los Angeles to find musical success.

"For these and other musicians, gigs and radio shows were one thing. Real success in the music business was quite another. And real success on their own turf seemed inconceivable," biographer Richard Younger wrote in *Get a Shot of Rhythm & Blues: The Arthur Alexander Story.*

"In a state without a [music] publishing company, songs could not be published," he added. "If there was no professional recording studio, you couldn't make a record. And in the latter half of the twentieth century, no record meant no real shot at stardom."

So it was in Alabama. But beginning in the late 1950s, everything changed.

1

THE SOUND OF
MUSCLE SHOALS

You ask me to give up the hand of the girl I love
You tell me I'm not the man she's worthy of
But who are you to tell her who to love?
That's up to her, yes, and the Lord above
You better move on.
—*"You Better Move On," Arthur Alexander (later covered by the Rolling Stones)*

Pore over books and historical records focusing on northwest Alabama, and the bulk of what you'll find will cover the Tennessee Valley Authority, a government-owned utility launched in Muscle Shoals in the 1930s. A 1950s Muscle Shoals Chamber of Commerce brochure indicated that the area had two radio stations, fewer than twenty-seven thousand residents and little to do (most of the listed activities—a football stadium, lighted baseball parks, playgrounds and so on—could have been based at area schools). It isn't until that decade that music started showing up in a significant way.

A man named Dexter Johnson can claim credit for the area's first recording studio, which he set up in his home in 1951. Johnson established a legacy not only for the region but also for his family; his nephew Jimmy Johnson grew up to become the Muscle Shoals Rhythm Section's guitarist. The younger Johnson's studio now sits cater-corner from his uncle's garage studio.

Although Dexter Johnson's initial forays into recording began in the earlier part of the decade, Shoals music didn't hit the professional level until 1956. Tune Records was a partnership formed by James Joiner, Kelson Herston,

Muscle Shoals, circa 1933. *Library of Congress.*

This photograph of the Muscle Shoals Bridge appeared on a 1950s-era postcard published by Dexter Press. *Auburn University Libraries Special Collections & Archives Department.*

A 1940s postcard of the Wilson Dam in Muscle Shoals, Alabama. *Author's collection, Aero-Graphic Corp.*

Above: A postcard of Wheeler Dam in the Shoals area of Alabama. *Author's collection, Anderson News Company, Florence, Alabama.*

Right: The first-known recording studio in the Shoals (shown here in the picture hanging on the wall at the Alabama Music Hall of Fame) was at the home of Dexter Johnson, who is remembered at the Alabama Music Hall of Fame. Johnson was the uncle of Muscle Shoals Rhythm Section member Jimmy Johnson. *Author's collection.*

This recording studio was built by Dexter Johnson in his garage in Sheffield and was the first in the Muscle Shoals area. Johnson, a member of the Blue Seal Pals, built the facility after he retired from the group and began working for the Tennessee Valley Authority.

BLUE SEAL

songwriter Walter Stovall and attorney Marvin Wilson. The studio focused on pop and country music, including songs written by Phil Campbell's Billy Sherrill and Franklin County's Rick Hall.

"It may not have been Nashville or Memphis, but the music scene in Florence was suddenly a reality, and everybody was hungry for a hit," Younger wrote.

When Percy Sledge, a hospital orderly at the time, came calling in 1966, though, Joiner sent him elsewhere. Sledge's sound, which he developed by humming while working in cotton fields, didn't jive with the more pop-sounding music of Tune Records, and so he turned to Norala Sound Studio. Rick Hall, who by then owned FAME Studios, let his friend Quin Ivy borrow his rhythm section for the recording of "When a Man Loves a Woman." The song went to number twenty-two on *Billboard*'s Top 100 for the year and attracted other talent to the Shoals area. It was later covered by artists such as Michael Bolton, Rod Stewart and Bette Midler.

But the region's music business had a long way to go before it attracted such big-name talent. First, the local folks needed to find a bit of success. Perhaps because of the region's proximity to Nashville, Tennessee, area musicians would often make the pilgrimage to the country music capital. But the demos they would tote were sometimes cut back at home. A local radio station helped musicians recording those demos as they sought songwriting careers. The quality was iffy, but the tapes sometimes brought the songs to the attention of bigger recording artists. In 1957, teenager Bobby Denton recorded the Joiner-penned "A Fallen Star" at Tune Records and began to see some success.

"It became a regional hit, almost a big hit," then Alabama Music Hall of Fame executive director David Johnson recalled in an interview with the *(Mobile, AL) Press-Register*. Denton, who later became a state senator, has noted that it is believed to be the first song recorded commercially in Alabama.

That inspiration was all it took for other aspiring musicians to jump in. Others saw Tune and Norala's success and decided to pursue their own music industry dreams. In 1958, Tom Stafford teamed up with Joiner, who was mostly a silent partner, to form the record label Spar Music Company. Spar Music opened in 1959 and also began working to create demos to draw attention from Nashville. Stafford, Billy Sherrill and Rick Hall also opened FAME Recording Studios in 1960. The partnership dissolved soon after, with Hall retaining the name. Stafford retained the studio, artists and recording label. Spar eventually disappeared while FAME became the stuff of legends.

"They said I worked too hard," Hall said to the *(London) Telegraph*. "So they fired me. They were thinking, by the time we get to 40 we ought to be millionaires. My thinking was, by the time I'm 30 I'll be a millionaire."

Hall used money loaned to him by used-car dealer Hansel Cross, whose jingles he recorded to open a new studio. Hall also married Cross's daughter, Linda.

In 1961, a bellhop named Arthur Alexander traveled the short distance from Spar to Hall's FAME Studios and made history. Stafford at Spar recognized that Alexander's song "You Better Move On" had real potential, but in the previous business partnership, Stafford had not overseen the business aspect of recording. Spar remained focused on demos. So instead, Stafford sent Alexander to Hall to record a polished version of his song.

It was the song that put the Muscle Shoals region on the musical map. When he couldn't find a label to release the song, Hall put it out on his own. The song traveled up the charts to number twenty-four. (A year later, the Rolling Stones would cover the song on the band's debut EP. That was before the group became one of the greatest bands of all time and well before it traveled to the Shoals to record its own work.) Within a few years, the *Playground Daily News* noted in a 1970 article, Hall had turned a $5,000 investment into a $1-million-per-year success story.

Hall subsequently built the current FAME studio, modeled after Nashville's RCA, and set to recording. Even in those early days, his stationery and the building's exterior predicted success, with "Home of the Muscle Shoals Sound" emblazoned on both.

"The Shoals had its first homemade hit record, and its first homegrown star," Lawrence Specker wrote in the *(Mobile, AL) Press-Register* in 2001. "It also had a recording boom on its hands: Once it had been proved that a hit record could be made in Alabama, any number of people were willing to try it."

And so they did.

There aren't any books specifically about Muscle Shoals…there are chapters.
—former Alabama Music Hall of Fame curator George Lair to the
(Mobile, AL) Press-Register

2
BECOMING FAMOUS

What you want
Baby, I got it
What you need,
Do you know I got it?
— *"Respect," Aretha Franklin*
Recorded with the Muscle Shoals Rhythm Section at FAME Studios

This is the story of Muscle Shoals Sound Studio. But you can't tell the story of Muscle Shoals Sound without FAME.

Rick Hall might have been in the right place at the right time when he ended up with the rights to the FAME name. But he began preparing for a career in music years earlier. Hall, a Mississippi native raised in rural Alabama, began writing songs and playing string instruments (especially guitar and mandolin) as a teen but didn't pursue a life in music until after his wife and father died. He began writing songs with Billy Sherrill before the pair went into business with Tom Stafford at Spar.

After he formed FAME, Hall continued to write and record music. While working with musician Jimmie Hughes, Hall wasn't certain the song they recorded, "Steal Away," was going to be successful. Rather than finding a label for it, Hall opted to release the song himself. Its success—as well as hits like hospital orderly Percy Sledge's "When a Man Loves a Woman," recorded with some of Hall's players at Quin Ivy's nearby studio—led to steady interest in the Muscle Shoals sound.

FAME Recording Studios was established in 1959 and moved into its current location in the early 1960s. *George F. Landegger Collection of Alabama Photographs in Carol M. Highsmith's America, Library of Congress, Prints and Photographs Division. Gift, George F. Landegger, 2010 (DLC/PP-2010:090).*

And the interest included that of Atlantic Records, which, at the time, was renowned for its soul recordings and ended up releasing Sledge's hit. Atlantic producer Jerry Wexler had established his credentials as well; while he was a writer for *Billboard*, Wexler introduced the phrase "rhythm and blues." When fellow Atlantic producer Joe Galkin told Wexler he must check out a rhythm section in northwest Alabama, Wexler was initially skeptical. He insisted he needed to hear evidence of the group's power before he would record there.

Percy Sledge's "When a Man Loves a Woman" was proof enough that something special was happening in this corner of the state. "The song was Percy Sledge's 'When a Man Loves a Woman,' a transcendent moment in the saga of Muscle Shoals, a holy love hymn that shot to No. 1 and made me realize Galkin was right: I had to get with Hall in a hurry," Wexler wrote in his autobiography. The song spoke for the region as a whole.

"A record just walked in here that's gonna make our whole year," Wexler reportedly said.

So perhaps it wasn't surprising that Wexler brought Wilson Pickett to Alabama in 1966, the same year Sledge's hit was released. Pickett had previously recorded at Stax in Memphis, but the studio had since closed its doors to outside artists. That meant Atlantic Records–based Pickett was in need of a new location. Besides, some reports indicate that Wexler thought his artists could benefit from a change of scenery. An article that later appeared in the *Huntsville (AL) Times* quoted Wexler as saying, "Some sort of atrophy had set in by the middle '60s. Just everything was running down because all the juice went out of the New York scene in that musicians were all out of licks and the arrangers were all out of ideas."

Maybe this northwest corner of Alabama held the solution, Wexler thought. After the original players moved to Nashville in 1964, FAME's new—and soon-to-be-legendary—rhythm section formed. Jimmy Johnson stepped in on guitar. David Hood took up the bass in tandem with Roger Hawkins's drumming, and after Spooner Oldham left for Memphis, Barry Beckett found himself at home behind the keys. Those musicians helped set the tone for "When a Man Loves a Woman," unwittingly setting themselves up for a long-term relationship with one of the recording industry's most legendary producers.

That rhythm section found great success at FAME. Their predecessors recorded a number of memorable songs ("Steal Away" by Jimmy Hughes and "Hold What You've Got" by Joe Tex, to name two), and the new rhythm section would continue that tradition.

In fact, the studio's reputation grew to the point that at least one musician would camp in the parking lot, desperate for a chance to play. Eventually Rick Hall took pity on that guitar player, and Duane Allman (later of the Allman Brothers) began his musical career.

Studios then operated differently from now. "We had no headphones in those days. There was a red light that came on and there's no 'talk back' in the studio. It's because of those circumstances that, it wasn't a challenge, but I think it made it more authentic," FAME keyboardist Spooner Oldham recalled in an interview with music blog Birmingham Box Set.

And the Muscle Shoals Rhythm Section's reputation as working in a fashion similar to that of Stax made it appealing to Wexler. He later wrote in his autobiography that the rhythm section was magic in the studio. Guitarist Johnson tore it up, he wrote; Wexler described drummer Hawkins as "sure-footed and naturally inventive…especially adept at sound consistency, especially soulful with the sock cymbal and bass drum"; and Oldham, who was still the group's keyboardist at the time, was a wizard. *Rolling Stone* later said Pickett's "rough, rusted vocals were right at home in the loose country funk" of the Shoals.

"Before Wexler," Hawkins recalled in Wexler's autobiography, "things were pretty quiet around the Shoals. Spooner Oldham and Dan Penn had written 'I'm Your Puppet,' which became a big hit for James and Bobby Purify, and there were a couple of other items, but not many. Jerry put the national spotlight on us. When Wexler said he liked my playing, well, that was a big moment in my life."

According to Johnson in Wexler's autobiography:

> *When Jerry started producing Pickett, he saw that our style allowed him to get involved in the rhythm section. He became part of the rhythm section.*

He loved that. He loved coming out of the control room and helping us find grooves. Maybe in New York he wasn't so loose with the musicians. He liked our Southern hospitality, and he could feel we were honored to have him down here. The combination worked—his get-it-done personality and our being laid-back. He got us organized—in and out, cut the tracks, do the vocals, mix it down. We gave him the relaxed feeling he wanted, and Pickett gave him hits.

Pickett recorded two iconic tracks, "Land of 1,000 Dances" and "Mustang Sally"—the latter written by Memphis-based Stax Records songwriter Mack Rice, who was previously part of the Pickett-fronted group the Falcons—with the FAME musicians. The latter song ranked 434th when *Rolling Stone* magazine ranked the 500 best songs of all time in 2004.

"'Mustang Sally' nearly ended up on the studio floor—literally. After Pickett finished his final take at FAME Studios in Muscle Shoals, Alabama, the tape flew off the reel and broke into pieces. But engineer Tom Dowd calmly cleared the room and told everyone to come back in half an hour. Dowd pieced the tape back together, saving one of the funkiest soul anthems of the Sixties," the magazine explained.

It wasn't the last time Pickett saw success at FAME either. Hall one day called Wexler so thrilled with Pickett's cover of the Beatles' "Hey Jude" that he insisted on playing the recording over the phone. "The vocal was fabulous, but it was the guitar solo, a running obbligato over and under Wilson's impassioned cries, that held the whole thing together. I knew all the session guitarists, but not this guy. So who was he?" Wexler wrote.

The guitarist, who Wilson had nicknamed "Sky Man," either because of his proclivity for drugs or happy-go-lucky nature (depending on who you ask), was Duane Allman. Allman had pestered Pickett into attempting the cover. But Pickett didn't agree until Allman started picking the song and the rest of the FAME musicians joined in. The cover spent six weeks on the *Billboard* charts, and Pickett put his own rhythm-and-blues inflected spin on the "na-na-na" refrain, tearing it up vocally with soulful cries.

Hall had, through this and other tracks, established a reputation for the blues. That served Wexler again when he brought Aretha Franklin to Alabama in 1967.

Franklin was twenty-four and had already cut her teeth on pop music at Capitol Records. But Atlantic believed she had more to offer. As Franklin took her seat at the piano in FAME, the band members rushed to keep up with her.

"I've never experienced so much feeling coming out of one human being," Roger Hawkins said, according to a story in *Rolling Stone*.

Aretha Franklin may have recorded only one song—the hit "I Never Loved a Man (The Way I Love You)"—in town, but Alabama left an indelible mark on her music. It was Franklin's sole trip to Alabama; her then husband, Ted White, and Hall became argumentative at the motel after drinking. Verbal barbs led to a physical fight.

According to Hall, after he was forced from the room, "I went downstairs and got on the house phone and I started screaming at the top of my lungs, 'You son of a bitch; if you come down here I'm gonna beat your damn ass.' Then Wexler came down the hallway, yelling and screaming, 'I told you not

Aretha Franklin recorded only one full song in Alabama, the title track of *I Never Loved a Man (The Way I Love You)*. But the Muscle Shoals Rhythm Section recorded on her albums for years to come. I Never Loved a Man (The Way I Love You). *Atlantic, 1995, originally released in 1967.*

to come over here, now you've ruined our relationship with Aretha. I will never record with you again, and I will bury your ass,'" Hall recalled to the *(London) Telegraph.*

It wasn't the first sign of tension between the two; Wexler had hoped for a racial mix and soulful contribution on the Franklin recordings and asked Hall to bring in a black horn section. Hall instead hired an all-white group, and Wexler was disappointed.

The session ended with the work only partly complete.

"For Atlantic Records, it was well worth the expense of flying Muscle Shoals players to New York to finish the album. These same guys played on Aretha's next three albums, traveling to New York each time. The courtiers for the Queen of Soul were white guys from rural Alabama," Carl Wiser and Nicholas Tozier wrote in an article for *Songfacts.* Those sessions included one of Franklin's signature songs, "Respect," which *Rolling Stone* dubbed the fifth-best song of all time.

"Otis Redding wrote 'Respect' and recorded it first, for the Volt label in 1965. But Aretha Franklin took possession of the song for all time with her definitive cover, made at Atlantic's New York studio on Valentine's Day 1967," the magazine wrote. "'Respect' was her first Number One hit and the single that established her as the Queen of Soul. In Redding's reading, a brawny march powered by Booker T. and the MG's and the Memphis Horns, he called for equal favor with volcanic force. Franklin wasn't asking for anything. She sang from higher ground: a woman calling an end to the exhaustion and sacrifice of a raw deal with scorching sexual authority. In short, if you want some, you will earn it."

The review continued, "And since Redding's version had no bridge, Wexler had the studio band—the crew from Muscle Shoals, Alabama, that had cut Franklin's Atlantic debut, 'I Never Loved a Man (the Way I Love You),' a month before—play the chord changes from Sam and Dave's 'When Something Is Wrong with My Baby' under King Curtis' tenor-sax solo."

The result of that first session, "I Never Loved a Man (The Way I Love You)," clocked in at number 186 on the list, and Franklin's "Do Right Woman—Do Right Man" also landed her at the 473 spot.

Although the Alabama–New York arrangement worked, the White and Hall argument that ensured Franklin would never return to Alabama might have sounded the death knell for Wexler and Hall. The influx of musicians would continue for some time, but Atlantic—and Wexler—would become a crucial part of Muscle Shoals Sound's history.

3

THE SWAMPERS

There's something happening here
What it is ain't exactly clear
—*"For What It's Worth," written by Stephen Stills and originally recorded by*
Buffalo Springfield; covered by Cher on her album 3614 Jackson Highway

Roger Hawkins, David Hood and Jimmy Johnson were already recording at FAME well before keyboardist Barry Beckett came along. Hood and Johnson's relationship dated back to high school in the Shoals region and extended to their time as students at the University of North Alabama (then called Florence State College). Johnson was studying retail, although his dream was to work in music.

After a gig in Jackson, Mississippi, fellow musician Dan Penn challenged Johnson. "He said, Johnson, why are you still going to college?" recalled Johnson, who was then in his junior year. "I said, 'Well, Dan…the only thing I can tell you is, if I don't make it in the music business, I'll have something to fall back on.' It was two minutes almost of silence. Finally, he said, 'Johnson, I know you.' He says, 'If you have something to fall back on, you'll fall back.' And you know what, he was right. I quit."

But Birmingham-born Beckett initially met Johnson and Hawkins at the University of Alabama, where they were playing with their band the Del Rays. Beckett was the right fit after Spooner Oldham left for Memphis in 1967—although the rest of the guys weren't immediately willing to admit it.

"When we first brought Barry into the rhythm section, he had some pretty big shoes to fill," Hood said to the *(London) Independent* on the occasion of Beckett's death in 2009. "We gave him a tough time at first, but soon he was kicking our butts and inspiring us to a greater level of musicianship."

After getting to know them, Jerry Wexler described the players who became known as the Muscle Shoals Rhythm Section as "Alabama white boys who took a left turn at the blues." Three of the four musicians were natives of the area, and even as the outsider, Beckett's Birmingham home was merely 115 miles away.

In 1969, Rick Hall was prepared to sign an exclusive deal with Capitol Records, and he decided to offer the group of musicians a guarantee of $10,000 a year. "We were already making more than that working with all these different people, but he wanted to sign us to an exclusive agreement for $10,000 a year, and we thought, well, that's not going to work," Hood said to *Songfacts*.

The Muscle Shoals Rhythm Section had established a strong working relationship with Atlantic producer Wexler, whom the members got to know through their work with Aretha Franklin and who produced Ray Charles. (Wexler would later count numerous other successful acts, including Bob Dylan and George Michael, among his clients. Both of those men would go on to record at Muscle Shoals Sound Studio.) As the musicians grew frustrated with Hall's low rates and controlling tendencies, Wexler stepped in.

The band might never have made the move to its own studio had it not been for Wexler's support. He offered the group financial assistance, including the purchase of an eight-track machine and financing for a second one, and he also guaranteed a steady stream of work.

"I found Rick Hall's supervision far too severe; he was impatient and treated the musicians like pawns," Wexler wrote in his autobiography.

And so in 1969, the group that would go on to be nicknamed the Swampers left FAME to open its own studio at 3614 Jackson Highway in Sheffield, the next town over. Wexler was president of Atlantic Records at the time, and the eight-track recording machine he helped the musicians purchase would work with Atlantic's existing equipment. He also invested more than $10,000 and ensured that Muscle Shoals Sound would see a steady stream of Atlantic's artists for the next eighteen months.

"The historic venture marked the first time that a cohesive core group of studio musicians—now known as the Muscle Shoals Rhythm Section—embarked on a multi-dimensional music venture that include joint ownership of a recording studio and publishing company," notes the

One of the studios where the Muscle Shoals sound originated. Singer Cher and other famous singers of the '60s recorded at this studio. *George F. Landegger Collection of Alabama Photographs in Carol M. Highsmith's America, Library of Congress, Prints and Photographs Division. Gift, George F. Landegger, 2010 (DLC/PP-2010:090).*

website of the Alabama Music Hall of Fame, into which the rhythm section members were inducted in 1995.

The group informed Hall of its intentions when he brought the members in to talk about the Capitol Records deal.

"Rick was Record Producer of the Year the next year with a new rhythm section. So he saw that he could do it without us," Hood recalled in an interview with *Bass Player* magazine. "But that's when we knew that we were a unit. When we left him and got our own studio, we knew we'd better get good."

The cement block building to which the group relocated had previously housed Fred Bevis Recording, which recorded demo tapes on a four-track. Johnson had helped Bevis set up the studio, where its namesake hoped to record country musicians. Johnson and Hawkins were friends with Bevis, a music minister, who talked them into buying the studio when his wife asked him to get out of the industry. They brought Beckett and Hood into the deal, and the rhythm section remained united.

But the venture needed a name. The group toyed with a number of ideas before Hood suggested Muscle Shoals Sound. The guys laughed;

after all, what was the Muscle Shoals sound? There was a Motown sound and a Nashville sound, but the words "Muscle Shoals sound" hadn't yet been defined. The town itself isn't even the largest of the Shoals region; that distinction belongs to Florence. The studio isn't located within Muscle Shoals; its address was in Sheffield.

"You have to live here to know when you're in one or the other, because there are places where you can stand with one leg in one and one leg in the other. But only people that live here really know where those spots are," Hood said to *Songfacts*.

Even so, the name stuck. The musicians knew Hall was upset with them for leaving FAME, and he hoped the new venture would fail. "So I thought, let's call it Muscle Shoals Sound just to get at Rick," Hood recalled to *Songfacts*. Over time, the phrase became best known as a reference to the blend of rock, rhythm-and-blues and country music for which the area's studios became known.

I think [Muscle Shoals] *has a "soul" more than a "sound." Older musicians and music historians talk about the "feel" of the music that came out of the studios in their heyday. Many of the bands there now have that feeling in their music.*
—independent artist manager and booking agent J.D. McCorkle to the
(University of Alabama) Crimson White

The studio itself is emblematic of the era in which it was built. The concrete and stucco building, erected in the mid-1940s, has changed little since its construction. Air conditioning and other modern conveniences have been added, of course. But otherwise it appears very much like the place where musicians such as Bob Dylan stepped outside for impromptu jam sessions. The unimpressive building is emblazoned with its address, 3614 Jackson Highway, which has become a siren song to many in the music industry.

The interior of the studio was only slightly more impressive than its basic exterior, even in its heyday. The former blinds factory had been reconfigured so that it included a recording room, a control room and two offices upstairs, with a bathroom wedged between the drum and guitar booths. At one time, the reception room's walls were lined with gold and platinum albums, awarded for selling 500,000 and 1 million copies of the recordings, respectively. (The Muscle Shoals Rhythm Section created more than fifty such hits at the studio.)

Fabric draped on the walls elsewhere for sound isolation earned the studio the nickname "burlap palace." The red oak floor also influenced the sound; its gentle inward slope deflected standing sound waves in the recording process. In the basement, two small echo chambers added to the recording experience while a recreation room gave artists a place to unwind.

With new bands in the studio nearly every week, the Swampers and the studio musicians with whom they worked had to become incredibly versatile. "The strong points of Muscle Shoals were the willingness on the part of the musicians to work, their improvisational talents, and arrangers like Barry Beckett and Clayton Ivey," Alabama Music Hall of Fame curator and former music writer Dick Cooper explained to swampland.com. "The musicians built their reputation on being willing to take whatever time was necessary to cut a hit, while in Nashville, the three-hour session was sacred. Muscle Shoals sessions would run late into the night if necessary."

Although the studio was home, the Swampers' projects weren't limited to efforts in the Shoals. Hood recorded with Santana on *Havana Moon,* Johnson worked with Billy Vera and the Swampers as a whole backed a variety of artists, including B.B. King and Johnny Mars, at the Montreaux Festival blues show.

"Like Ray Charles, B.B. had grown a little complacent with his routine band, and I figured my Alabamians would kick some ass," Wexler wrote. "I was right. B.B. loved them; that night Switzerland sizzled."

There were clear differences between FAME and Muscle Shoals Sound, though, most importantly that FAME was a production studio and Muscle Shoals Sound was, at its inception, a tracking studio. That meant that Hall would spend weeks with the artists who came his way, working on their albums from start to finish. At Muscle Shoals Sound, a different producer arrived nearly every week.

"Every Monday morning, we've got a new artist and a new genre of music," Johnson recalled years later.

Dick Cooper learned that the hard way when he wrote a music column for the *Florence Times–Tri-Cities Daily* (now the *TimesDaily*) in the early 1970s. Each week, he reported who was in town and where they were working. It made sense to him to focus on new arrivals.

"While this seemed like the obvious way to handle the column, it didn't take into account the differences between the two principle studios, FAME and Muscle Shoals Sound," Cooper recounted in an interview with swampland. com. "I was oblivious to the fact that when Rick recorded an act, he did it from start to finish. During pre-production, he would meet with the artist, review the material, and select the songs to be recorded."

Since Hall spent five or six weeks with each act, he made the top of Cooper's column only once every month and a half or so. Hall thought that unfair, and when Cooper's column moved to *Billboard* magazine, Hall decided he wouldn't stand for it. A call to the editor resulted in Cooper being fired. (Decades later, Hall recommended that the Alabama Music Hall of Fame board of directors hire Cooper as the executive director's assistant. He later became the museum's curator and developed most of the exhibits on display.)

Over the years, though, Cooper learned a great deal about the industry. He ultimately left journalism for the music business, where he worked as Barry Beckett's assistant, a road manager, a photographer and, now, a music museum curator.

The Swampers' ultimate goal, though, was to move into production, and so the distinction between the two studios didn't last.

There were admittedly hard feelings between the rhythm section and Hall after the former left to open its own studio. "It was war. Total war," Hall recalled in the documentary *Muscle Shoals.* "He said, 'You're never going to make it,'" Hood said.

But those issues ultimately worked themselves out, and the Shoals-area studios proved the old adage "a rising tide lifts all ships." *Billboard* magazine dubbed Hall the world's best producer in 1971, proving he was just fine without the rhythm section. His new band, the FAME Gang, was the studio's first biracial group and quickly carried on the FAME legacy.

"I was in the middle of the war, and it didn't really help anybody," Rick Hall's son Rodney said with a laugh. Years later, everyone was on good terms, often working together to promote both studios through the Muscle Shoals Music Foundation, of which the younger Hall served as board chair. "We all love one another. I never had a problem with the Swampers."

Hall received a Grammy for lifetime achievement in 2014, and hometown paper the *(Florence, AL) TimesDaily* named him the newsmaker of the year in 2013, the year the documentary *Muscle Shoals* drew eyes and ears back to the region. Hall's remarks at the time indicated how far his relationship with the Swampers had come.

"I know I probably shouldn't, but I would like to speak for all of us—the Jimmy Johnsons, the David Hoods, the Roger Hawkins, the Barry Becketts, the Norbert Putnams and all the guys that were there before, and for the FAME Gang—without them, we could not have accomplished as much as we did with hit records," Hall said in an interview with the *TimesDaily*. "With Muscle Shoals Sound, if you took their music out of the mix, Rick Hall would not amount to as much."

4

THE SINGING RIVER

And I will lay my burden down
Rest my head upon that shore
And when I wear that starry crown
I won't be wanting anymore
—"Take Me to the Mardi Gras," Paul Simon

S t. Augustine, Florida, has Ponce de Leon's Fountain of Youth. And so it stands to reason that Muscle Shoals, Alabama, must have an equivalent: a fountain of creativity.

Or so it would seem. What else could account for the wealth of hit songs and albums that poured forth from here, especially in the 1960s and '70s?

"There's this force that comes out of the ground," musician and Shoals transplant Scott Boyer said to the *Birmingham (AL) News*. "I don't know how else to explain all this great music that comes out of a little Podunk town in Nowhere, Alabama."

In 1980, the *Birmingham (AL) Post-Herald* offered as an explanation "the high quality of most of the area's studios and the willingness and ability of local musicians to work longer and harder than other areas' musicians."

Topography and geology are at least partially responsible for developing the Shoals; limestone in the Tennessee River created reefs—also called shoals—which drew mussels, giving the city its name. (How, exactly, "Mussel"

Wilson Dam and powerhouse in Muscle Shoals, circa 1933. *Library of Congress.*

became "Muscle" is a source of great debate. In letters to newspaper editors in the 1930s, Alabama residents reacted strongly to editorials in the *Huntsville Times* and the *Birmingham News* that discussed the spellings. Whether "muscle" is an acceptable, alternate spelling for "mussel" or the area was so named for the muscle required to navigate its waters, readers clearly had well-defined opinions on the matter.)

The Wilson Dam harnesses the river—which some also say is shaped like a muscle in an arm—and created a number of jobs through the Tennessee Valley Authority. The area's previous residents, the Chickasaw Native American tribe, referred to the Tennessee as a "singing river," and they believed there was magic in those waters. The river's song varies based on the water levels, but it always creates an enchanting melody.

"We used to sit out on the back stoop at night watching the lightning bugs dance around the cemetery across the street and that lent some magic and mystery to the atmosphere which seemed to permeate the music that was made there," musician Johnny Townsend said to *Songfacts*.

"At certain times on this planet, there are certain places where there is a field of energy," Jimmy Cliff said in the 2013 documentary *Muscle Shoals*. Cliff, a Jamaican-born reggae artist, should know. He recorded his 1971 album *Another Cycle* at Muscle Shoals Sound.

But some scoff at the idea that the city provides some sort of magic. FAME founder Rick Hall is among that number.

"They believed—they really believed—that we were cutting hit records because there's a special air here or there's a moon beam that hits this country on the northern border or there's a mist from the river drifting over here," he said to the *Birmingham News*'s Bob Carlton when the reporter sought answers to what made this area so special. "We made it in Muscle Shoals in spite of Muscle Shoals, not with the help of Muscle Shoals."

Carlton ultimately concluded that the secret ingredient was the people: Hall, Jimmy Johnson, David Hood, Roger Hawkins, Barry Beckett; the many stars who came to town; other studio musicians who called the area

In the *Muscle Shoals* documentary, reggae artist Jimmy Cliff said, "At certain times on this planet, there are certain places where there is a field of energy." Another Cycle, *Island Records, 1971.*

home; Jerry Wexler and other producers who sent business to the northwest Alabama towns; and songwriters who peddled their wares in these studios.

Wexler wrote in his autobiography:

> *The magic was in the music and the music was so deeply ingrained in Muscle Shoals—in guitarists like Eddie Hinton, keyboardists like Spooner Oldham, songwriters like Donnie Fritts. Music was in the air you breathed and the water you drank, coming at you so inexorably and naturally that I found myself returning to the place not simply a few more times but on dozens of occasions over the next quarter-century. More than any other locale or individual, Muscle Shoals changed my life—musically and every which way.*

A list of Shoals-area recording studios, past and present, at the Alabama Music Hall of Fame. *Author's collection.*

That geography also influenced the sonic qualities of the music, which mixed sounds that were considered white and black, country music with soul and rhythm and blues.

"You can draw a triangle from Nashville to Memphis to Muscle Shoals, and while Nashville is the country center, Memphis is generally known as the blues center," then Alabama Music Hall of Fame curator George Lair said to NPR. "Muscle Shoals, being between those two places, has been able to combine those two styles into a real southern rhythm and blues that was very appealing."

At one point, the local music industry included about a dozen studios and employed more than one hundred people in some fashion. *Billboard* estimated the area was responsible for 20 percent of the singles and albums on its charts in the early '70s.

"I told my dad over the years, and I told David and those guys: if they'd never left you, this would have been a one horse town. It would never have been as big as it became," Rodney Hall, son of FAME founder Rick Hall, said to *Songfacts*.

But the studios' success stories were about more than the people, crucial as they were, and the competition that sometimes fueled them. The studios themselves also influenced the music that came out of the region.

"It's a 100-year-old red oak floor. The building is a little twisted, which is really cool, because there's no standing wave in the building, there are no parallel surfaces. And the room is incredibly bright and sounds gorgeous," Noel Webster, who owned Muscle Shoals Sound's original home, 3614 Jackson Highway, from 1999 to 2013, said to *Songfacts*. "So any way you stick a mic, you don't get standing waves, and it's just a wonderful thing."

Such "fingerprint sound" rooms were more common during the studio's most successful period from 1969 to 1978, with albums from Sun Studios and others bearing an unmistakable sound. They were places "where you hear a record on the radio and know immediately where it was cut," Jimmy Johnson explained in an interview with *Sound on Sound*.

That unusual construction combined with the rhythm section's top-notch musicianship to create an unmistakable sound. "Musicians, when they play, have a sound just like somebody's voice has a sound," Hood said to *Songfacts*.

Likewise, Hall set a precedent at FAME. His setup emphasized bass and drums, and he was relentless in recording. Hall didn't care how many takes it took, he was determined to get what he was seeking out of his musicians.

"Back then we emphasized probably the bass and the bass drum more than anybody else did and just had what they call funk sound, and it became known as the Muscle Shoals sound," then Alabama Music Hall of FAME director David Johnson said to Weekend Edition.

And although the studio musicians weren't necessarily trained to read music, the resulting style of their playing changed everything. The rhythm section would write out chord charts by numbers, rather than using each chord's name. This left a lot of room for improvisation and experimentation. That, too, had been established at FAME. The studio's producer and engineer Jerry Masters said most of the area's musicians felt the music, rather than reading it. Masters himself could relate; his producing skills relied on similar intuition. "I know what sounds right to me," he told the *Florence Times*, "but I couldn't tell you all the technical ends of this board or this job."

There is immense poetry in the way those records were made and the depth of those records. The sound of David Hood's bass playing—it seems to go with the name Muscle Shoals. Yet there is sparseness and economy of playing, which is a hallmark of soul.
—Say It One Time for the Broken Hearted *author Barney Hoskyns in an interview with the* TimesDaily, *March 11, 2001*

"When the boys came in Monday afternoon, they'd get a copy of the chord chart and would start to pick. They'd play around, maybe lock into a lick, find a nourishing groove, feel their way into a structure," Wexler wrote in his autobiography. "Someone might develop an especially tasty rhythm line—maybe a two-bar syncopated pattern, an outstanding turnaround, or a provocative fill. The arrangement would build communally and organically. The ideas could come from anyone."

And rhythm was everything—as you might expect from a region that prized its rhythm sections. Any supplementary instruments could be added as needed, but hitting the rhythmic groove was key and rhythm section musicians were given plenty of space for creativity.

In those days, a flubbed note would make its way onto the final recording. "Nowadays you fix everything. Nothing is real," Hood said to *Songfacts*. And that authenticity was a key part of the sound.

"Digital is great but it gives you a different sound," then studio manager Suzanne Harris said in an interview with the (Mobile) *Press-Register* in 2001. "Analog is better for the blues."

Johnny Sandlin, who was the producer at the time of the interview, said the studio kept the magic alive even in the twenty-first century by recording to analog tape. Muscle Shoals Sound producers would then use digital technology to refine the work.

As the music scene developed, the region also became a hotbed for local talent. "In the Shoals, if you needed a hired gun to come in and knock out some part for your song, whether it be guitar, bass, drums, horns or whatever, you just pick[ed] up the phone and call[ed] one of your friends to come over and lay it down for you. It was a kind of community environment you can't get in the big recording centers," Johnny Townsend of Sanford-Townsend Band explained to *Songfacts*.

The attitude of those musicians was also more focused and dedicated than in the music industry centers, or so said Music Mill studio president Al Cartee in a 1977 United Press International interview. "None of the studio musicians who lives here ever comes in and says, 'Oh, God, I've got to cut a session.' That just doesn't happen here like it does some places," he explained. "They come in ready and willing to work. We don't work by a clock. We work all hours of the day and night until we get the sound we want."

Wishbone Studios owner Terry Woodford backed him up. In the same story, he said: "Our musicians care. Here when a singer books a studio, the musicians stay until they get the sound they're looking for. They play together, they communicate with each other."

That was also true of the folks behind the scenes. "All that equipment don't mean jack if you don't have the right guys turning the knobs," Johnny Townsend said to *Songfacts*.

And so, the Shoals area became *the* place to go for musicians who wanted to capture a certain sound. "I think they just got funkier records here than they did anywhere else," FAME studio president Rodney Hall said to NPR. "And it's a lot more laid-back than any other music center in the country."

"There is some soul in Alabama that you can't find in Los Angeles," Clarence Carter added to Hall's assessment.

Even so, some believe the phrase "Muscle Shoals sound" is a misnomer. "As a recording engineer, the idea of the 'Muscle Shoals Sound' is silly to me," Alabama Shakes keyboardist and Single Lock Records co-owner Ben Tanner said to the *(University of Alabama) Crimson White* in 2013. After the late '60s, Tanner said, the albums recorded in the area don't share sonic DNA.

Instead, he explained, an emphasis on excellence made the area stand out. That expectation has been passed through the generations. "It's less about being a flashy player and showing off what you can do with a solo and more about 'How can I make this song good? What's my role? What's my part to play in this song?'" Tanner said. "The song is the real center and focal point."

It's the feel for the music that made the area's musicians stand out, the *Birmingham News* asserted in 1971.

"The people working together in the Muscle Shoals music industry comprise a unique fraternity of individuals, highly skilled, creative and in pursuit of a common goal, the production of recorded music—principally rock or 'soul'—for consumption in the international market," Bob Bates wrote in a 1971 article for the *Birmingham News*. "Here one will find songwriters, musicians, vocalists, producers, publishers, engineering technicians, blacks, whites, all striving in conquest of the magic that is literally gold—a gold record that denotes the selling of one million singles or albums by any artist or group."

Whatever answer you believe, it seems that the Shoals region is the perfect confluence of factors to make it a musical hotbed.

"There's [*sic*] beautiful things out there, and magical things. This place, for whatever reason, just emanated music and had a certain energy to it. And it seems to have emanated that for a long time, and I think that was obviously complimented [*sic*] by driven people," filmmaker Camalier said to *Rolling Stone*. "The coming together of races at that time, as well as the landscape and this rural, beautiful town, as well as the singing river, as well as these incredible characters and all the other musicians down there—it all sort of came together."

5

A SLOW START

So take a letter Maria, address it to my wife
Say I won't be coming home, gonna start a new life
—*"Take a Letter, Maria," R.B. Greaves*

R ight off, the Swampers faced difficulty in their new space. Although FAME's location wasn't glamorous (today, it's located by a CVS drugstore), it was more spacious and was built to be a studio.

Muscle Shoals Sound, however, was a converted commercial building. "A loud truck driving down the street or a heavy rainstorm, you'd have to stop working, because it was not built as a studio," David Hood said to *Songfacts*. Limited space also meant limited options for renovating the studio.

The studio opened on April 1, 1969, and the early days were a struggle. "At first, it was death," Hood said to the *Birmingham News*.

Cher was one of the first big-name acts to record at the fledgling studio. But the resulting album, *3614 Jackson Highway*, did not see widespread success. It was composed largely of covers and peaked at 160 on the *Billboard* chart. Jerry Wexler had intended his voice to have the final say in each decision, and he was able to select the majority of the album's songs. But Wexler ended up in the hospital before the recording began and was unable to return to the control room before the project's end.

When Cher came to the studio in 1968, Sonny and Cher's careers were in a tailspin. Their last hit had been years earlier, as had the raven-haired singer's last solo hit. So Atlantic Records decided to try something different

The cover of Cher's *3614 Jackson Highway*, one of the first albums recorded at Muscle Shoals Sound Studio, includes a photo of the musicians who played on the album. *Front, left to right*: guitarist Eddie Hinton, bassist David Hood, Sonny Bono, Cher, producer Jerry Wexler, background vocalist Jeannie Greene, background vocalist Donna Jean Godchaux and producer Tom Dowd; *back, left to right*: lead guitarist Jimmy Johnson, producer Arif Mardin, drummer Roger Hawkins and keyboardist Barry Beckett. Background vocalists Mary Holiday and Sue Pilkington were not pictured. 3614 Jackson Highway, *Rhino, 2013, originally released in 1969.*

with Cher. Sending her to Alabama and pairing her with the Muscle Shoals Rhythm Section in its new environs, along with other album contributors, was an attempt to stretch her creatively.

Despite the lackluster chart position, some would say it worked. Take the AllMusic.com review, for example:

Cher was given some weightier material than she usually handled, including no fewer than three Bob Dylan covers and some classic soul numbers, and if "I Walk on Gilded Splinters" and "For What It's Worth" don't seem like ideal choices today, she sounds mature, forceful, and authoritative on every track. And while Cher doesn't quite come off like a soul diva on these sessions, she welcomes the opportunity to dig deeper into the songs in a way she couldn't on many of her early hits, and she rises to the challenge posed by her collaborators—she rides the slinky funk of "Lay Lady Lay" beautifully, knows just how to fill the quiet spaces of "Please Don't Tell Me," and belts out "Cry Like a Baby" with the same punch as the Memphis Horns. 3614 Jackson Highway was a commercial disappointment and it would be another two years before Sonny & Cher would return to the limelight with their television variety show, but Cher was rarely given a better showcase for her talents as a singer, and the album still sounds like a revelation four decades after it was released.

In 2003, Rhino Handmade rereleased the album—now considered a collector's item for those who can find the original—with updated liner notes and bonus tracks. Music historian and critic Richie Untenberger wrote an extended essay for the liner notes, revealing both the context in which the musicians recorded *3614 Jackson Highway* as well as its place in music history. He concluded:

Cher's record ended up as but the first of many by superstars in Muscle Shoals Sound, the Rolling Stones using it in late 1969 to record part of Sticky Fingers *there. And in terms of Cher's own career,* 3614 Jackson Highway, *despite its failure to become a big seller, possibly remains the most concentrated attempt to find the rootsiest and highest-class contemporary material and production for her vocal talents.*

Wexler's expectations again went unmet during some of the subsequent sessions, which took place from September to October 1969 with the artist Lulu. The 1970 release *New Routes* was also a disappointment. "They yielded only a mini-hit in 'Oh Me Oh My (I'm a Fool for You Baby),' which later was covered by Aretha," Wexler recounted in his autobiography. "Since Cher's record had produced no hits, for the most part I was striking out."

The band was hard at work, but the music coming out of Muscle Shoals Sound had yet to gain traction. "We didn't realize there was a big long back time till the first hit would come out," Jimmy Johnson said. "But we were booked every week for a year when we opened the door."

R.B. Greaves's "Take a Letter, Maria" was the first hit recorded at Muscle Shoals Sound Studio. R.B. Greaves, *Atco Records, 1969.*

Things heated up quickly come August 16, 1969.

Wexler's business partner, Ahmet Ertegun, showed up at the studio with singer-songwriter R.B. Greaves, who entered the studio ready to cut the soulful "Take a Letter, Maria." Ertegun stood in stark contrast to Wexler's more focused style; while in town, Ertegun bought cowboy boots, hung out in the studio and was so relaxed that he made the process seem easy.

And of course, "Take a Letter, Maria" helped. The song's horns give the lyrics (which detail the narrator's wife's adultery) an infectious, uplifting resonance.

The song raced to number two on the *Billboard* charts. "The whole thing was so easy I think it kind of bugged Jerry," Hood recalled in Wexler's autobiography. Six months after its opening, Muscle Shoals Sound had its first hit.

6

THE ROLLING STONES

I know I've dreamed you a sin and a lie
I have my freedom but I don't have much time
Faith has been broken, tears must be cried
Let's do some living after we die
Wild horses couldn't drag me away
— *"Wild Horses," Rolling Stones*

They really weren't supposed to be there.

The Rolling Stones pulled in to Sheffield, Alabama, on December 2, 1969. Two nights earlier, they had wrapped a thrilling performance in West Palm Beach, Florida. The band had a few days of downtime before their next big show—the soon-to-be-legendary Altamont performance in Los Angeles. The free show drew 300,000 fans to Altamont Speedway, and it was the site of four births and four deaths, including a stabbing death committed by a member of Hells Angels just in front of the stage.

But before they went on to make rock-and-roll history on Altamont Speedway, the band hoped to sneak in a little recording time.

There was a problem, though: Union complications and back taxes meant the Rolling Stones weren't actually supposed to be on a working vacation.

Not that it stopped anyone. Part of the appeal of recording in the Shoals, after all, was its out-of-the-way location, and the Stones had been assured their visit could be kept secret. A band could show up with British accents and flamboyant style and still go unrecognized.

The Rolling Stones spent several days in the Shoals in December 1969. The three tracks they recorded appear on *Sticky Fingers* and remain an important part of the band's repertoire. Sticky Fingers, *Universal Music Enterprises, 2009, originally released in 1971.*

After all, Muscle Shoals Studio was a nearly unknown entity. The owners had a little backing and plenty of talent, but there was only one hit to the fledgling business's credit—R.B. Greaves "Take a Letter, Maria." Cher's *3614 Jackson Highway*, the Muscle Shoals Rhythm Section's first attempt at working with a well-known artist under the auspices of its own studio, was a commercial nonstarter.

But the Rolling Stones, newly signed to Jerry Wexler's Atlantic, were something else. The British invasion had been dominating American airwaves, and the Stones' most recent album, *Let It Bleed*, was an emotional release that elevated the band from its previous work (and briefly knocked the Beatles' *Abbey Road* out of the top spot on British charts). With the Beatles on the cusp of releasing their final album, the Rolling Stones were arguably the best band in the world.

And the Muscle Shoals Rhythm Section was prepared. Jimmy Johnson was at the ready with the studio's Scully eight-track machine primed to roll tape whenever the band was set.

That's exactly what occurred during the Stones' three-day residency at Muscle Shoals Sound. The band spent the majority of its time in the studio, playing out its kinks before launching into new material. "The Stones came in, and they were a little rusty at first because they hadn't been practicing on account of the tour," Johnson recounted to BMI in 2009.

So the band would spend the first several hours of work on any particular song ironing things out, and Johnson would be poised. On night one, they recorded "You Gotta Move," a cover of a Mississippi Fred McDowell song. A review in *Rolling Stone* magazine would later cite this track as an album highlight, especially because of Mick Taylor's electric slide guitar and Richards's acoustic guitar and harmonies.

The band and session musicians spent most of day two ironing out wrinkles in their sound before settling in for the second evening's task. This time, as tape began rolling, the now famous strains of "Brown Sugar" filled the former blinds factory. The Chuck Berry–inspired song clocked in at 490 on *Rolling Stone*'s list of the top 500 songs ever recorded.

In that list, the magazine wrote, "Here the Stones lay waste to a battery of taboo topics—slavery, sadomasochism, inter-racial sex—and still manage to be catchy as hell. The song got its start at a session at Muscle Shoals studios: Jagger scrawled three verses on a stenographer's pad, and Richards followed with an impossibly raunchy riff. Add some exultant punctuations ("Yeah! Yeah! *Woooo!*") and you have a Stones concert staple."

Day three was equally—if not more—successful. At one point, Keith Richards began ruminating over what would become the song "Wild Horses." His son had been born four months earlier, which made being on the road difficult. After Richards jotted down the chorus in the studio's small bathroom, Jagger polished the lyrics. He left only one line of Richards's original work, but it sticks with listeners: "Wild horses couldn't drag me away." Between Richards's inspiration and Jagger's finesse, the Rolling Stones walked away with what would go on to become one of the band's signature songs. Richards added a guitar riff, and "Wild Horses" was born.

Richards heard Jim Dickinson, a Memphis studio musician whose sons Cody and Luther are now two-thirds of the North Mississippi AllStars, noodling around on an old piano in the building as the band worked up the song. After Richards commented, Jagger declared Dickinson should play on the song—and so he did. "I got on 'Wild Horses' because Ian Stewart, their regular piano player, wouldn't play minor chords," Dickinson later recalled.

"In the meantime, they wouldn't be saying anything to me, but I knew I had to get the very best performance when it happened," Johnson said in the BMI interview. "After a few takes of 'Wild Horses,' Jagger just looks up at me and says, 'Is that it?'—like I'm the producer or something! But I knew when they had it—and I just told 'em to come out and hear it back.'"

Sure enough, the song went to number 28 on charts, and "Brown Sugar" hit number 1. Andrew O'Hehir wrote on Salon.com that the songs represented a new sound for the Stones—and one they never again created. *Rolling Stone* ranked the song number 334 in its list of the 500 best songs of all time.

"Richards wrote this acoustic ballad about leaving his wife Anita and young son Marlon as the Stones prepared for their first American tour in three years. Stones sidekick Ian Stewart refused to play the minor chords required, so Memphis musical maverick Jim Dickinson filled in on upright piano at the Muscle Shoals, Alabama, recording session for *Sticky Fingers*," the magazine wrote.

Despite the Stones' sometimes colorful reputation, they were professionals in the studio.

In his autobiography, Jerry Wexler noted, "As producers, they knew exactly what they wanted and how to get it. Their musicianship really came into play in the studio process. They controlled their craft and ran the whole show with dead-on direction. I was confabulated."

Nights later, when the Rolling Stones performed at Altamont, Jagger introduced the newly recorded "Brown Sugar." While the three songs the band taped during those three days all became part of *Sticky Fingers*, the Rolling Stones' first number-one album in the United States, "Brown Sugar" remains one of the band's most enduring songs.

And though the recording session would produce the band's first stateside smash, it wasn't as though the Stones were unheard of in Alabama. Even so, as the band lounged in the median of a Tuscumbia highway, watching and waving at passersby, locals seemed to accept them as nothing more than a passing curiosity. Bands weren't unusual in the Shoals, after all. But had they been recognized, having the Rolling Stones in town would have been newsworthy indeed. Imagine if the residents had realized who the odd-looking out-of-towners actually were!

It wasn't the only time the band went unnoticed. Instead, when a Holiday Inn waitress asked the fur coat–clad wife of then bassist Bill Wyman if the fellas were part of a group, Wyman replied they certainly were: Martha and the Vandellas.

"Their visit was kept a secret from most of the locals, and the world's biggest rock and roll band came, recorded and left (headed for infamy at Altamont, no less) without the conservative townsfolk even knowing they had been there," David Hood's son Patterson wrote in an essay for the *Bitter Southerner.* Some reports even suggest Hood sent his wife and son flying out of town to protect the band's anonymity.

I probably saw stuff I wasn't supposed to, did things I was told not to, and heard a lot of amazing music that I didn't fully appreciate for years. I had to protest my roots to come to celebrate them.
—Patterson Hood to the Winston-Salem Journal

The Rolling Stones remained unnoticed and soon left the Shoals for even greater success as their streak of number-one United Kingdom albums continued and they began the same for the States.

"There was something about the Muscle Shoals feel," Richards said to BMI later. "Charlie (Watts, drummer) really filled up that room with sound—it was so easy to cut in there." When interviewed for the documentary *Muscle Shoals*, he added, "I don't think we'd been quite so prolific ever."

The Stones would have returned to the Shoals to record their next album, *Exile on Main Street*, were it not for issues with their visas, Richards later said. Instead, the album was composed of tracks the band recorded while on the road in the States, at Jagger's home as well as in the basement of Richards's home in Nellcôte in the south of France. But the Shoals and Alabama in general will always be able to stake their claim on a piece of the Rolling Stones' legacy.

7

TIME TO KILL

I love my baby like a schoolboy loves his pie
Like a Kentucky colonel loves his mint 'n rye
I love my man till the day I die
— "St. Louis Blues," W.C. Handy

The same thing that allowed the Rolling Stones to walk around the Shoals anonymously and later sent the Black Keys out of town as quickly as they could wrap was part of what made recording in the area special: There wasn't much else to do.

"I remember one time a few years back when I went into a restaurant and there sat Sonny and Cher," then Muscle Shoals mayor "Shanky" Sharp recounted to the *Birmingham Post-Herald* in 1980. "I shook their hands. And do you know there were seven millionaires at that table? I tell you it's (music business) big."

Even so, the Shoals area remains quiet, out of the way and decidedly a non-industry town in the twenty-first century.

"The atmosphere in town is conducive to work," Muscle Shoals Sound public relations director Sharon Weiss said to the *Birmingham Post-Herald* in 1980. "Because there's nothing to do here but work. It's a dry county and there aren't any bars around."

"The things we did to overcome the fact that we were in the middle of nowhere," Dick Cooper said.

"We bought a beer machine," Jimmy Johnson said. "When the law found out we had it, the first question they had was, 'What do you charge for it?'

We said, 'We give it away.' 'You give it away?' And we said, 'Yeah, we don't charge for it.' They said, 'Then we don't have a problem with that.' They could only get you if you sold it. That was the only law."

In fact, in one of the most iconic photos taken at 3614 Jackson Highway, Jerry Wexler stands with Willie Nelson in front of the building with a pilsner glass in hand.

People ask, "Man, so what's it like, growing up in Muscle Shoals?" And I don't know. There's a Hardee's?
—*musician Browan Lollar, formerly of Jason Isbell and the 400 Unit, currently of St. Paul and the Broken Bones, paraphrased in a Birmingham Box Set blog post from an interview on Birmingham's Substrate Radio*

In 1971, Rick Hall told a *Florence Times* reporter: "Artists like to come here because they can relax. Actually there is nothing to do here but relax. You can't even have a beer unless you drive 19 miles to Tennessee." Even in 1980, that was a tried-and-true explanation. "All the things that stifle creativity just don't exist in Muscle Shoals," Lee Daley, assistant engineer at the area's Wishbone Studios, explained to the *Birmingham Post-Herald*.

Although the area is no longer dry, the dearth of entertainment options remains the case today. Interview a musician from rural Alabama, and it's likely that he or she will tell you boredom is at the root of the music. Brittany Howard of the Athens, Alabama–based Alabama Shakes told *Birmingham* magazine she began playing guitar at age thirteen to kill time. "I was trying to make musicians," Howard said. "I would take kids in my grade and tell them, 'You're going to learn to play bass guitar now. Play this!'"

And even with the resurgence of Muscle Shoals music in the 2000s, the region remains sleepy at best. Music blogger and area native Blake Ells wrote:

"Muscle Shoals" is Athens, Georgia, but it isn't self-aware. No one from Athens, Georgia, is afraid to tell you that they invented "college rock" or that they have 60 bars in two blocks. But folks from "Muscle Shoals?" Well, there's a CVS Pharmacy next door to FAME, the studio that a nobody named Duane Allman camped outside of for a month because he was desperate for Rick Hall to give him a chance. There's a used car lot in what was then La Fonda Mexican Restaurant, where folks like Jason Isbell, Chad Gamble, Jimbo Hart, Browan Lollar and Gary Nichols cut their teeth because they were too young to play at the other three "bars" in town. And there's a time when the W.C. Handy Music Festival, a week-

The W.C. Handy exhibit at the Alabama Music Hall of Fame in Tuscumbia includes a number of artifacts from Handy's career. *Author's collection.*

long celebration of Florence's native son, held concerts at the Red Lobster or Princeton's, a now-defunct restaurant that was essentially the same as any other O'Charley's or Applebee's.

The Alabama Shakes' Ben Tanner has also noted that the area's music history is based almost entirely on the recording studio. The musicians who elevated the area to the stuff of legend were focused on recording great music, not performing live.

Similarly, the Shoals became a recording haven because it provided an escape from outside pressures. The South generally moves at a slower pace, but there's more to the Shoals' success than its laid-back vibe. There were very few venues during the area's recording heyday, and they continue to come and go today. Colbert County was dry until 1981, and even today, Florence is a wet city in dry Lauderdale County. There wasn't an airport in town, and now the Northwest Alabama Regional Airport only offers flights to Atlanta. In the great tradition of rural areas, front-porch jam sessions were passed through the ages.

Although being isolated was one of the area's charms, it also created production challenges. While working on Bob Dylan's *Slow Train Coming*, Cooper recalled, "We had to have the day's mixes on the desk in L.A. the next day. And we would work till midnight. Now how do you get that tape to L.A.? Well, the way you do it [is] I would take it, I would drive to Huntsville to the Huntsville airport every night and [I would] put it on air freight to L.A." A courier would pick up the mixes at the airport and deliver them to the record label.

Spare time is our major export. Even though Muscle Shoals is a good-feeling place, there's not much entertainment, other than to make music.
—*Mac McAnally to the* Birmingham News

"We didn't have FedEx when we started, or UPS or nothin' like that," Johnson added. "I remember one time Wilson Pickett threatened us. We were finishing an album on him that he paid for. I was filing extra time to get the mix just perfect. He called me one day, and he said, 'If you don't have my album in New York by tomorrow, I'll kill you.' I said, 'Well, you won't have to do that because it'll be there.' They had counter to counter, so he had to go pick it up. But we'd send it to our airport counter to the counter there. That's the way we had to do it, but we could do it overnight that way."

"It survived against all odds," wrote music blogger Ells, who is from nearby Rogersville. "Good people wanted to make good music. And there are still a lot of good people here doing it."

Modern musicians agree. Laura and Lydia Rogers, known professionally as the Secret Sisters, have said they'll never make their home outside northwest Alabama. Being able to go unnoticed keeps them humble and offers a reprieve from the hectic pace of life on the road.

"One of the things I love most about that town is that nobody bothers you," Lee Roy Parnell said to the *Birmingham (AL) News*'s Mary Colurso. "We set aside a few days to lay down the basic tracks, and we didn't want any interruptions. It was kind of like we were in a bubble.'"

That continues to draw out-of-towners to the area, as well. "We would always get rooms at the Holiday Inn in downtown Florence and carpool it over to the studio and be talking about the music all the way. Because they didn't have the kind of distractions like New York or L.A. you could get much more focused, and because their studio rates were so much less expensive, you could block it out for days, or even weeks at a time and basically camp out in the studio," musician Johnny Townsend said to *Songfacts*. Or as writers Carl Wiser and Nicholas Tozier put it in the same article, "There was nothing to do in Sheffield but eat dinner and roll tape."

8

LYNYRD SKYNYRD

If I leave here tomorrow
Would you still remember me?
For I must be traveling on now
'Cause there's too many places I've got to see
—"Free Bird," Lynyrd Skynyrd

B y 1971, Muscle Shoals Sound and other area studios were not only drawing national and international recording artists to their sleepy corner of Alabama but also generating media buzz. In a March 1971 editorial, the *Birmingham News* wrote, "If the recording studios—there are several doing a profitable business—are locally-based, the recording stars who come from all parts of the country and from Europe to take advantage of the Muscle Shoals enterprises' growing reputation for coming up with hit songs and million-copy gold records have given flavor to the area." By 1980, the area accounted for more than four hundred such records.

One of those early sessions was with Lynyrd Skynyrd, then merely known on the Florida bar circuit. ("Leonard who?" Barry Beckett supposedly asked on the band's first visit.) Whenever the band could get a break, it hit the road for Muscle Shoals, where the band members slept in a shared truck stop room while recording their first album.

Recalling the sessions decades later, then drummer, now guitarist Rickey Medlock said to the *Huntsville Times:*

LYNYRD SKYNYRD

SKYNYRD'S FIRST

THE COMPLETE
MUSCLE SHOALS ALBUM

Although Lynyrd Skynyrd recorded its first album at Muscle Shoals Sound, the tracks weren't released till later in the band's career, after a plane crash killed several members. Skynyrd's First: The Complete Muscle Shoals Album, *MCA, 1998, originally released in 1978 as* Skynyrd's First and...Last.

> *Man, we were so green. It was the first time we'd ever been in any kind of major recording studio. We had basically no idea of what the reputation of Muscle Shoals Sound was or who had been here to record or anything like that. All of a sudden, we landed in there and worked with Jimmy and David and the guys. That's when we realized who had cut hits in there and how major this was for us. I give them credit for teaching us to record.*

Although Skynyrd's original Muscle Shoals session took place years before the band found success with its debut album, *(Pronounced 'Lĕh-'nérd 'Skin-'nérd)*, the project that became *Skynyrd's First and...Last* wasn't released until after the infamous 1977 plane crash that killed three band members, including lead singer Ronnie Van Zant. The delay was partly because the tape with the original recordings was kinked on its way to record labels.

"What 'Lynyrd Skynyrd's First and Last Album' is is a fine representation of the band's early years, and its transition from a Jacksonville, Florida, bar band into a professional rock group," *Rolling Stone*'s Dave Marsh wrote in advance of the album's release.

The album, which was rereleased in 1998 as *Skynyrd's First: The Complete Muscle Shoals Album*, includes the original cuts of "Free Bird" and "Gimme Three Steps."

One afternoon, the band returned to the studio after a lunch break to find Allen Collins playing a concert piano. Collins had long been tinkering with the chords that would become "Free Bird." But lead singer Ronnie Van Zant insisted the number of chord changes made it difficult for him to find a melody. On that afternoon, though, Van Zant heard something that struck him, and "Free Bird" spread its wings. The version that later appeared on *Skynyrd's First and...Last* clocks in at a mere seven minutes, but the song could stretch to as many as fourteen minutes in concert, when the jam session gave Van Zant's vocals a break.

This version of "Free Bird" admittedly lacks the soaring, driving melodies that make the *(Pronounced 'Lĕh-'nérd 'Skin-'nérd)* recording endure. Even though the original version of the iconic track is arguably less impressive, *First and...Last* is a worthwhile purchase. In his record review, *Rolling Stone*'s Marsh wrote:

> *Although it was recorded primarily between 1970 and 1972, this isn't just a relic for Lynyrd Skynyrd fans. One of the best albums the band ever made,* Skynyrd's First and...Last *ranks either a notch above (better material) or below (slightly poorer playing) its first two records,* Pronounced 'Lĕh-'nérd 'Skin-'nérd *and* Second Helping. *A triumphant but ironic final chapter, it measures the extent of the tragedy of the group's demise.*

The band itself reflected on the time spent recording the album with great nostalgia. In the liner notes for the reissued version, guitarist Gary Rossington wrote, "Even though we were from Jacksonville, Florida, the Muscle Shoals Swampers helped us so much that I think Lynyrd Skynyrd's whole career and music really are from Muscle Shoals, Alabama."

In 1997, Lynyrd Skynyrd returned to Muscle Shoals Sound. Although the lineup wasn't the same as the band's first visit in the '70s, Skynyrd was eager to return to the area where the band first recorded.

"Muscle Shoals was the first place we came to when we came out of Florida and started to make it," founding member Rossington explained to the *Huntsville Times*. "So we decided to come back to those roots. When we got here, I got a rental car and just drove all over town that afternoon. It was like seeing home again, and that was cool. The studio's great, we did a lot of albums here, the Swampers are here and so much great music came out of here. We love it."

By this time, the Sound Studio was in its second location, at 1000 Alabama Avenue. The resulting album, *Twenty*, commemorated the anniversary of the plane crash that killed Ronnie Van Zant, Steve Gaines and Cassie Gaines.

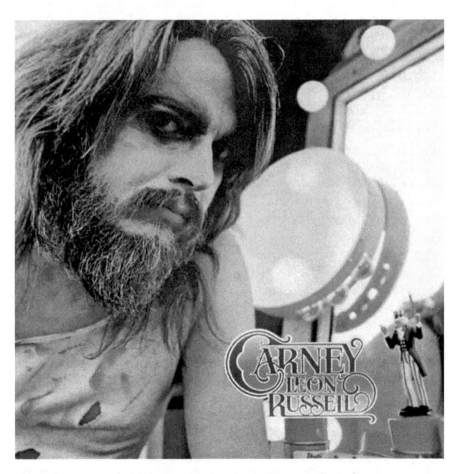

The Muscle Shoals Rhythm Section's nickname, "the Swampers," is said to have originated during a session with Leon Russell, but it became well known thanks to Lynyrd Skynyrd's "Sweet Home Alabama." Carney, *Shelter, 1972.*

The band finalized the album in Nashville and then released it on April 29, 1997. One of the songs from that album, "Travelin' Man," made a 1997 list of five Muscle Shoals songs featured in the *Huntsville Times*.

Although the musicians at Muscle Shoals Sound had by this time long been known as the Muscle Shoals Rhythm Section, it wasn't until Leon Russell recorded his album *Carney* at the studio in 1972 that they became known as the Swampers. The nickname, coined by producer Denny Cordell, describes the music the rhythm section created, which always evokes the sticky southern air and swampy environment.

And Lynyrd Skynyrd immortalized that name. The band's most famous Muscle Shoals tie wasn't recorded in Alabama at all. In the state's unofficial

Lynyrd Skynyrd's *Skynyrd's First and…Last*, later reissued as *Skynyrd's First: The Complete Muscle Shoals Album*, achieved platinum status. *Author's collection.*

theme song, "Sweet Home Alabama," Ronnie Van Zant sings, "In Muscle Shoals they've got the Swampers, and they've been known to pick a song or two." If the Denny Cordell–created nickname hadn't already stuck, Van Zant and his crew ensured the Muscle Shoals Rhythm Section would forever be known as the Swampers.

Jimmy Johnson recounted a conversation with Ronnie Van Zant to the *Huntsville Times* in 1999: "He said, 'Jimmy, we just cut a song about you.' Little did I know…," Johnson said.

And how could he? Although the band is from Jacksonville, Florida, and the song was recorded in Doraville, Georgia, Skynyrd remains a beloved Alabama icon, and "Sweet Home Alabama" is many folks' first introduction to the musical region.

9
THE STAPLE SINGERS

I know a place
Ain't nobody cryin'
Ain't nobody worried
Ain't no smilin' faces
Mmm, no no
Lyin' to the races
—"I'll Take You There," the Staple Singers

Finding a steady stream of talent became more difficult for Muscle Shoals Sound in 1971, when Atlantic moved its business to Miami's Criteria Studios. But Memphis-based Stax Records saw its own troubles as bad business decisions took a toll, and that became a boon for Muscle Shoals Sound. Stax needed to turn out as much music as possible, and so the studio's executives decided to send some of the artists to Alabama.

The Staple Singers were among those bands. The group had previously recorded in Memphis, and the Shoals proved a fit for the act's gospel-inflected crooning.

But it wasn't a choice the group's producer and Stax co-owner, Al Bell, found easy to explain to his friends and family. He had already been criticized for locating in Memphis, Tennessee. People told the Arkansas-born Bell that Memphis wasn't the right place to build a music career; rather, he should focus his efforts in one of music's major cities.

Working in the Shoals was met with an equal lack of enthusiasm.

The Staple Singers found success with their producer, Al Bell, while recording *Be Altitude: Respect Yourself* in the Shoals. Be Altitude: Respect Yourself, *Concord Music, 2011, originally released in 1972 by Stax Records.*

"That music that you all are doing down there, that 'Bama music'—they put a negative connotation on the music and a negative inference as it relates to Alabama, 'Bama, and all that," Bell explained to the *Arkansas Review*.

His history with the Staple Singers dated back to a call from the Reverend Jesse Jackson. Bell worked at Little Rock radio station **KOKY** at the time and was taken aback when he heard the group. "I mean, the harmonies were not like anything I'd ever heard," he recalled years later in an interview with the *Arkansas Review*.

Bell recounted his conversation with Jackson in that interview, as well. Jackson said, "You need to take Mavis and Pops and go in the studio and produce them yourself. I don't think nobody can produce them but you. Unless you do that, then they're not going to get the kind of shot they should get. You need to take them under your wing yourself as a producer." And so Bell did.

Muscle Shoals Sound proved the right fit for both Bell and the Staples. In a 2005 interview with *Harp* magazine, he recalled, "The chemistry that developed between me and those guys was amazing. I felt really comfortable down there 'cause they welcomed me with open arms. And the chemistry between them and the Staples was just pure magic, man. They felt the Staples so easily, felt what Mavis was trying to do as a singer and the hits just rolled out."

Working with the Staple Singers provided new opportunities for the Swampers, as well. In 1972, David Hood and Roger Hawkins joined the British band Traffic on tour. ("It wasn't an immediate, easy marriage," Traffic's Steve Winwood later said to filmmaker Freddy Camalier. "I was forced to learn how to jam," Hawkins said.) Traffic's interest had been piqued by Jamaican reggae and ska artist Jimmy Cliff's album *Another Cycle*, recorded at Muscle Shoals Sound. "Jimmy brought a bunch of Jamaican records with him—old ska singles, by the Upsetters and groups like that," Hood later recounted to ProSoundWeb's Bruce Borgerson. "We were amazed by that sound, and it showed us a few things, like the ways to turn the beat around. It planted a seed with us."

While on tour with Traffic, Hood and Hawkins were exposed to even more reggae; Bob Marley's *Catch a Fire* had just been released, and it played in advance of Traffic's performances every night. That out-of-the-studio experience diversified the Swampers' influences, and they took those sounds home to the Shoals.

But it wasn't until the rhythm section recorded with the Staple Singers that those influences surfaced on a recording.

When he arrived in Sheffield, the Staple Singers in tow, Bell was able to talk music and build relationships unlike he had elsewhere. When he entered the studio, Bell would talk through what he wanted to hear, and then the rhythm section would translate it to music. He had an especially strong working relationship with Barry Beckett, who would work through Bell's notes on the piano and then translate his desires for the rest of the group.

It may not have been a traditional arrangement, but it worked. The Staple Singers recorded their biggest hit at Muscle Shoals Sound.

Just before the group went to Muscle Shoals, Bell learned that his brother had died. As he mourned his brother's death, lyrics popped into his mind: "I know a place, ain't nobody worried, ain't nobody crying, and ain't no smiling faces, lying to the races."

In addition to recording on Traffic's *Shootout at the Fantasy Factory*, several of the Swampers toured with the band. Shootout at the Fantasy Factory, *Island, 1973*.

"Well, I was a little fifteen-cent writer there, and I said, 'Wait a minute; I've got to have more words. I don't have enough verses.' And I kept trying to write other verses, but I couldn't. Nothing worked. There was nothing left to say," Bell said to *Arkansas Review*.

When the band arrived at Muscle Shoals, those lyrics were the last track to be recorded. Bell had fleshed out the song with "ohs" and "ahs"—crying out, he said, in response to the loss he felt.

At first, Mavis Staples couldn't feel the music. Bell sang it to the rhythm section, and as the musicians played it back to him, they captured his vision. But Mavis took longer to come around.

"After getting it down, later on I came back and sat with Mavis, and after a while, she started feeling it and giving in to that rhythm. Of course, she…took it to heights that only a Mavis Staples can take it," Bell said. "Only Mavis, only Mavis. Nobody else could do it justice, and I guess it was supposed to be that way."

Bassist David Hood also had a moment to shine in that song. Mavis Staples sings out his name at 1:52 in the song, and he responds with a solo. "That *Be Altitude: Respect Yourself* album is one of my favorites of all time," Hood said to *Bass Player* magazine. "The Staple Singers were fun, too. Three sisters and Pops—we just had a good time with them."

The Muscle Shoals sessions resulted in "I'll Take You There," which went to number one, and "Respect Yourself," a number-twelve hit; the album on which the songs appeared, *Be Altitude: Respect Yourself*, hit the number-three spot on *Billboard*'s soul chart and went as high as nineteen on the pop chart. And in 1972, Stax offered the rhythm section royalties on any subsequent sessions recorded at the studio. Estimates on just how many sessions that eventually included range from 50 to 80 percent of the record label's 1970s catalogue.

10

WHERE BLACK AND
WHITE MEET

Respect yourself, respect yourself
If you don't respect yourself
Ain't nobody gonna give a good cahoot
—*The Staple Singers, "Respect Yourself"*

Although the Shoals music industry was at its height in the years immediately following the civil rights movement—which saw many tide-turning events take place in Alabama—race relations weren't a hot topic in the studios. When Greg "Freddy" Camalier came to town to film his *Muscle Shoals* documentary, which was released in 2013, he initially thought the musicians he interviewed were downplaying the issue. But as conversations continued, he developed a better understanding of how black and white comingled.

"Three-quarters of the way through an interview and every musician, black and white, will tell you there was a lot of good energy, good vibes in Muscle Shoals and that was a key to making it special," Camalier said to *Billboard* magazine. "It played a role in the sound and, when you think of the context, of where you are in the country, it gives you a lot of respect for all of those guys."

Such hot topics showed up in the music, too. Jerry Wexler noted that Aretha Franklin's "Respect" touched not only on sexuality—which is perhaps a more obvious reading of the song's lyrics—but also civil rights and integration. The influence of such black musicians on Alabama white boys was tremendous—and of course, David Hood has noted, you couldn't tell someone's skin color by listening to a song on the radio. (The Muscle Shoals Rhythm Section would later see that in reverse, as many people assumed the musicians who backed Aretha Franklin, Wilson Pickett and others were black.) The *Philadelphia Inquirer* would go on to note, "But to hear (Clarence) Carter tell it, when it came to skin color and race relations inside FAME (it stands for Florence Alabama Music Enterprises), everyone was as blind as he."

Although it wasn't what they had grown up with, David Hood, Jimmy Johnson, Roger Hawkins and Barry Beckett couldn't resist the appeal of rhythm and blues.

"It was like a salty chili dog after years of Patti Page and Perry Como," Wexler once said to *Sound on Sound*. "And it became the progenitor of rock 'n' roll."

Such music found success in fraternity parties throughout the South, such as those at the University of Alabama, where Johnson and Hawkins met while playing in bands. "At the University of Alabama, if you didn't play the Moonglows' Mama Loochie they'd whip your ass," Johnson explained to the *(London) Telegraph*.

"I could see that Southern whites liked their music uncompromisingly black," Wexler wrote. "Despite the ugly legacy of Jim Crow, their white hearts and minds were gripped, it would seem, forevermore."

For the Muscle Shoals Rhythm Section, though, what happened in the studio was merely about the music. "We hated to go home," Johnson said to the *TimesDaily*. "Working was what excited us." All that mattered was the quality of work, not the skin color of the person making it.

Likewise, Lynyrd Skynyrd's "Sweet Home Alabama" (which name-checks Muscle Shoals although it was recorded elsewhere) delved into racial tensions. "By referencing Muscle Shoals, a small city on the Tennessee River in northern Alabama, and the Swampers, an all-white rhythm section who played on some of the greatest R&B records ever made, the Skynyrd songwriters were attaching themselves, however covertly, to the tradition of race-mixing and cultural ferment that is the greatest source of strength and vitality in American culture," Andrew O'Hehir wrote in a 2013 Salon.com review of the documentary *Muscle Shoals*.

O'Hehir's analysis of the film and its subject matter dove deeply into the implications of a white studio band recording with black soul singers.

"Of course white privilege was involved, because even though Rick Hall grew up dirt-poor, he still belonged to the class of people who were able to buy property and start businesses in 1950s Alabama, and he hired white musicians—at least at first; his post-Swampers bands were integrated—because it was the natural thing to do," O'Hehir wrote. "All that said, Hall's also a guy with a tremendous ear and immense soulfulness who knew what he wanted—and what he wanted was a sound that fused Delta blues, hillbilly and urban African-American music. And something geographical or historical or spiritual about that obscure river-bend in northern Alabama made that possible."

The result might not be perfect, O'Hehir concluded, but it shows another side of the civil rights story: a place where everyone could come together. Some argue that the country influence on R&B music was the key ingredient for Shoals-recorded music's crossover success. Whatever the case, the resulting music has proven longer lasting than the segregationist attitudes that then prevailed in other arenas.

That influence continues to show up in the region's music. Drive-By Truckers, which formed in 1996, often identify as an Athens, Georgia band, but the founders hail from the Shoals area. One of them, Patterson Hood, is the son of Muscle Shoals Sound's David Hood.

The band's 2001 album *Southern Rock Opera* is "equal parts Skynyrd tribute and autobiographical vignettes from Truckers lead singer Patterson Hood," the *Mobile Register*'s Joe Danborn wrote. The Hood-penned spoken-word piece titled "The Three Great Alabama Icons" explores the influence of George Wallace, Ronnie Van Zant and Bear Bryant. (The latter two weren't from Alabama, but their sway—one a member of Lynyrd Skynyrd, the other the legendary University of Alabama football coach—is unmistakable.)

The song explores the dichotomy between a South that embraces Lynyrd Skynyrd but doesn't realize that the band idolized Neil Young, the very singer about whom they sang "a southern man don't need him around anyhow."

"Bands like Lynyrd Skynyrd attempted to show another side of the South, one that certainly exists. But few saw beyond the Rebel flag," Hood says in the song.

"In my song, I discussed the dualities of being from a region that is known for great music and literature and art and something called 'Southern hospitality,' but is also known for Jim Crow laws, slavery, racism and the Ku Klux Klan," Patterson Hood wrote in an essay for *Bitter Southerner*. "I talked about being fiercely proud of the good parts of my heritage and mortified and ashamed of the bad parts, the ones that too often define how other people perceive us."

In fact, some argue that the colorblindness that seemed to exist in the recording studios was exactly what made Muscle Shoals studios so successful. "It was the combination of black and white that made the music work—black artists and the famed, all-white Muscle Shoals Rhythm Section," *The Muscle Shoals Sound* producer Randy Poe said to the *Huntsville Times* when Rhino Records released his compilation in 1993.

11

THE HIT PARADE

Just take those old records off the shelf
I'll sit and listen to 'em by myself
Today's music ain't got the same soul
I like that old time rock and roll
—*"Old Time Rock and Roll," Bob Seger*

The hits kept coming, both to the blues- and rock-focused Muscle Shoals Sound and to FAME, which recorded a number of top-selling pop musicians, including Paul Anka and the Osmonds. The Swampers had quickly seen their investment pay off. A 1971 *Birmingham News* article reported that they earned between $25,000 and $40,000 each in the studio's first year, and the production company raked in more than $150,000. Jimmy Johnson estimated that, for a time, 10 percent of the songs on *Billboard*'s Hot 100 charts were recorded at Muscle Shoals Sound.

The Swampers set themselves up for success by becoming more than guitars for hire. The guys always had a song ready when an artist needed one, with songwriters on staff. That allowed them to build up a publishing business.

"So we got a song on nearly every album we did, and that's how we built our publishing company, was by getting songs on albums that people were coming in to record," bassist David Hood said to *Songfacts*. In the '70s, Muscle Shoals Sound Publishing Co. president Terry Woodford said as much to the *Florence Times*: "Our studio is set up so that anyone who works hard and really makes a substantial contribution to the success of the studio becomes part owner."

It's important to note that, although these four musicians were the studio's founders and owners, they were far from the only Shoals-based session players on these albums. Guitarist Pete Carr served as lead guitarist for much of the studio's work and also recorded extensively at FAME. His musical fingerprints cover many of the records Muscle Shoals Sound recorded, from Bob Seger to Boz Scaggs and Paul Simon to Rod Stewart. He also found success as a music engineer, record producer and composer. Carr was predated by Eddie Hinton, a Jacksonville, Florida native whose playing was included on records by the Staple Singers, Cher, R.B. Greaves, Wilson Pickett and many other musicians whose work helped make the Shoals legendary. The Shoals sound is a product of a number of collaborators, not only the men who owned the studios and kept them running. Shelves could be filled with stories of those who shaped the area's music scene.

I was always enthralled by Muscle Shoals—the Memphis sound, Stax Records and Muscle Shoals. If I was going to make a record, that's where I was going to make one. —actor and musician Billy Bob Thornton to the Birmingham News *(Thornton recorded an album at the Shoals-based Widget Sound when he was eighteen.)*

Following the local industry's success, a group of local music business folks formed the Muscle Shoals Music Association in 1974. The world was already well aware of the music coming out of the area—even if they didn't know that this corner of Alabama was responsible for much of it—but Shoals residents didn't always recognize that these efforts were coming from their hometown.

The association worked to change that by partnering with the chamber of commerce—which, as recently as the early 1970s, was reluctant to support the music industry for fear of the type of person it would attract.

"Muscle Shoals—The Hit Recording Capital of the World" soon showed up everywhere, from the iconic city limit sign to city stationery and police cars. According to a 1982 *Mobile Press-Register* article, the ratio of gold singles and albums to recording sessions was higher in the Shoals than anywhere else in the world. At least 25 percent of the songs recorded at FAME in 1970 charted, and estimates from the time indicated that Muscle Shoals Sound wasn't far behind.

"Studios are kind of like mushrooms around here. Some pop up after every rain," Shoals-based journalist Dick Cooper said to Richard Younger in his book *Get a Shot of Rhythm & Blues.* Although Muscle Shoals

Musician Martin Colyer by the "hit recording capital of the world" sign. *Martin Colyer.*

Opposite, top: Boz Scaggs initially came to the Shoals posing as a *Rolling Stone* journalist. Later, *Rolling Stone* publisher Jann Wenner produced Scaggs's album at Muscle Shoals Sound. Boz Scaggs, *Atlantic, 1990, originally released in 1969.*

Opposite, bottom: Luther Ingram recorded "(If Loving You Is Wrong) I Don't Want to Be Right" at Muscle Shoals Sound Studio. (If Loving You Is Wrong) I Don't Want to Be Right, *Stax, 1972.*

Sound and FAME remain the best-known Shoals studios, they were kept company by Broadway Sound (previously named Quinvy Studio), Cactus, Wishbone, East Avalon, Widget, Dixie Recorders, Paradox and more. And Muscle Shoals' client list continued to grow, adding on such famed acts as Willie Nelson (*Phases and Stages*), Paul Simon (*There Goes Rhymin' Simon*), Bob Seger (*Night Moves* and *Stranger in Town*), Boz Scaggs (*Boz Scaggs*; the musician initially showed up masquerading as a *Rolling Stone* writer and eventually returned to record his album with Rolling Stone publisher Jann Wenner co-producing), Traffic (*Shoot Out at the Fantasy Factory*, which Roger Hawkins and David Hood played on during Jamaica recording sessions, and *On the Road*, recorded live, just as the name implies), J.J. Cale (*Really*), Joe Cocker (*Luxury You Can Afford*), Joan Baez (*Honest Lullaby*) and more. In 1975 alone, the studio hosted Rod Stewart (*Atlantic Crossing*), Johnnie Taylor, Paul Simon and Art Garfunkel (both together and individually) and Peter Yarrow of Peter, Paul and Mary.

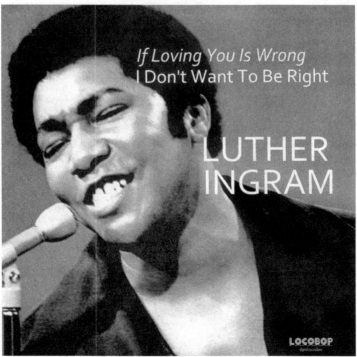

Mary McGregor was among the many artists who spent time in the Shoals. Torn Between Two Lovers, *Ariola Records, 1976.*

Joe Cocker's seventh album, recorded at Muscle Shoals Sound in the 1970s, features a number of cover songs, including "I Heard It Through the Grapevine." Luxury You Can Afford, *Asylum Records, 1978.*

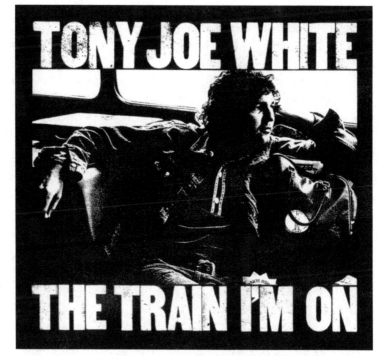

Tony Joe White recorded *The Train I'm On* at the studio in 1972. The Train I'm On, *Warner Brothers, 1972.*

The soul duo Mel and Tim's "Starting All Over Again" spent nine weeks on the *Billboard* chart in 1972, peaking at number nineteen. Starting All Over Again, *Stax, 1972.*

David Hood later said he had dreamed of success in New York when he was younger, but he realized he loved being home.

"Most places you have to go to New York, L.A. to get in the business. The unique thing that happened was they came to us. At the time, we didn't know how important that was. We realized we didn't like to travel or do live, on the road. We did get to travel around the world, but not every day," Johnson said. "People didn't come here to tell us what to do. They mainly came here for what arrangements we could give them."

Why should the rhythm section move the operation when they were content and bands would flock to them?

> *When I think back*
> *On all the crap I learned in high school*
> *It's a wonder*
> *I can think at all*
> —*"Kodachrome," recorded by Paul Simon*

And flock they did. When Simon arrived in Alabama, he was in search of the black musicians who gave the Staple Singers' "I'll Take You There" such energy.

"I don't know the exact story, but either Paul or his manager called Al Bell (owner of Stax Records) and said he wanted to record with the black Jamaican musicians who played on 'I'll Take You There,'" Hood recalled in an interview with *Bass Player*. "As I understand it, Al said, 'I can give you their number, but they're "mighty pale."'"

Simon, like so many others before and after him, was surprised to find a bunch of white guys behind the sounds he so admired.

"Muscle Shoals was the place to get that 'swampy' sound and singers came from as afield as France or Japan and were amazed to find four Caucasians," Pierre Perrone of the *(London) Independent* recalled in Barry Beckett's obituary.

That wasn't the only surprise Simon found at the Sheffield studio. The roof was leaking above the recording console, and the musicians had gotten creative with their solution. They taped feminine sanitary pads across the ceiling to prevent rainwater from reaching the console.

"So we had Paul Simon, who's got hit record after hit record walking in and seeing this place with Kotex on the ceiling," Hood recounted to *Songfacts*. "He must have thought, what in the world have I gotten myself into?"

Paul Simon's *There Goes Rhymin' Simon* includes five tracks recorded at Muscle Shoals Sound: "Take Me to the Mardi Gras," "Kodachrome," "One Man's Ceiling Is Another Man's Floor," "St. Judy's Comet" and "Loves Me Like a Rock." There Goes Rhymin' Simon, *Columbia, 1973.*

The feminine products weren't the only ad-hoc way the Swampers worked to keep moving. In order to muffle the sound of raindrops, the musicians lined the bottom of the buckets they set out to catch the drips with toilet paper.

Regardless, the visit was a success. Simon arrived in the early '70s, with four days reserved in the hopes of recording "Take Me to the Mardi Gras." But he was surprised by the results; the rhythm section nailed the song on the second take.

Of course, that meant he had studio time to spare, and it wouldn't be going to go to waste. Simon put the Swampers to work. In all, the musicians

Paul Simon came to Muscle Shoals Sound expecting to record one track. After wrapping it up quickly, he went on to record several others, including the hit "Kodachrome." Kodachrome *(single), Columbia, 1973.*

appeared on five tracks on the resulting 1973 release *There Goes Rhymin' Simon*: "Take Me to the Mardi Gras," "Kodachrome," "One Man's Ceiling Is Another Man's Floor," "St. Judy's Comet" and "Loves Me Like a Rock" (performed with the Dixie Hummingbirds).

"He was amazed, though, because he has always taken so long recording things, he couldn't believe that we were able to get something that quickly," Hood recounted to *Songfacts*.

The results were a hit. "Like its predecessor, it is a fully realized work of art, of genius in fact, but one that is also endlessly listenable on every level," *Rolling Stone* wrote in its review. "The chief new musical element Simon has chosen to work with—one he has hitherto eschewed—is black music: R&B and gospel motifs are incorporated brilliantly both in Simon's melodic writing and in the sparkling textures of the album's ten cuts, more than half recorded in Muscle Shoals, Alabama."

And the numbers backed up that assessment. "Kodachrome" and "Loves Me Like a Rock" both went to number two on the *Billboard* charts.

> *But you're gone and I'm alone and I'm still livin'*
> *I don't like it but I'll take it till I'm strong*
> *And all I can hear myself singin*
> *Is, I still can't believe you're gone*
> —*Willie Nelson, "I Still Can't Believe You're Gone"*

Many artists came to the Shoals seeking the musicians that made it famous, as Paul Simon did. But Willie Nelson turned his attention to Alabama at Jerry Wexler's suggestion. Some industry folks expressed surprise when Wexler suggested Willie Nelson travel to the Shoals to record 1974's *Phases and Stages*. "They [Nashville industry folks] said Muscle Shoals was too R&B for Willie; I said Willie was too R&B for Nashville," Wexler wrote in his autobiography.

But Nelson himself was open to the change of scenery. Nashville's reputation for expecting country music to fit a specific mold was already well established; after all, Elvis Presley had slipped right through Nashville's fingers.

Phases and Stages, recorded with the rhythm section's backing, is a conceptual album that explores the end of a relationship, first through a woman's eyes and then through a man's. It is, of course, a subject with which Nelson was well acquainted.

The album didn't see a single chart, but it was beloved by critics. *Rolling Stone*'s Chet Flippo summed it up this way: "The fact that Nelson can fashion a believable scenario with such sparseness is a tribute to his ability to turn experience into good music. *Phases and Stages*, his best work to date, now seems to call out for the filmmaker who can turn good music into good cinema." In another story, this one for *Texas Monthly*, Flippo argued that the term "concept album" was a misnomer for *Phases and Stages*; "I would call it a musical documentary," he wrote.

Country music critic John Morthland expanded on the concept and the context in which the album was recorded in his book *The Best of Country Music*:

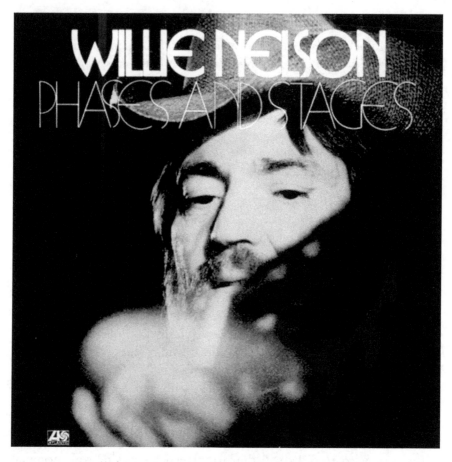

Willie Nelson's *Phases and Stages* is a concept album that dissects a relationship. Producer Jerry Wexler argued that Nelson was too R&B for Nashville, and therefore Muscle Shoals was the perfect place to record the effort. Phases and Stages, *Atlantic Records, 1974.*

Nearly everything about the album represents a departure. It was recorded at Muscle Shoals, Alabama, using primarily the same session musicians who cut much of the great soul music of the late sixties and early seventies; it was produced by Jerry Wexler, who made his name working with R&B and soul artists from the fifties and sixties. The album is also rife with contradictions; it's got more jazz inflections than anything Nelson had done, yet it's also true to his Texas country roots (he was born in Abbott in 1933). Finally, this is a concept album that sounds good whether you're listening to the words or not.

Although the album didn't achieve gold status, it was the beginning of something special for Nelson. After its release, he was able to negotiate a CBS Records contract because of the critical reception. Nelson also saw a streak of platinum records in the years that followed.

But even in the midst of a hit-making and career-inspiring streak, not all artists were so fortunate with their Muscle Shoals efforts. In 1975, Art Garfunkel and his Simon & Garfunkel partner Paul Simon simultaneously released solo albums. Simon's, *Still Crazy After All These Years*, merited Grammy awards for Album of the Year and Best Male Pop Vocal Performance. The album, which featured David Hood, Barry Beckett and Roger Hawkins, also

Art Garfunkel's *Breakaway* was the artist's second solo effort. It hit number nine on the *Billboard* 200 chart. Breakaway, *Columbia Records, 2008, originally released in 1975.*

featured four top-forty hits. Of those, "50 Ways to Leave Your Lover" hit number one.

Garfunkel's *Breakway*, on the other hand, wasn't as critical a success.

"I Only Have Eyes for You" peaked at number eighteen, and "Break Away" ascended only to number thirty-nine. *Rolling Stone*'s Dave Marsh didn't hold back in his review:

> Breakaway *is certainly superior to* Angel Clare *the first Art Garfunkel solo album. But it's difficult to decide how much the singer had to do with its success, aside from having the good sense to choose Richard Perry to produce it. Releasing the album in conjunction with Paul Simon's may have been commercially advantageous—particularly since "My Little Town," the S&G reunion, is included on both—but artistically it is an error of incalculable proportions. After hearing these two records side by side as they've been offered, who can doubt that Simon really is the artist. Garfunkel only the simple production tool?*

> *I am sailing, I am sailing,*
> *Home again cross the sea.*
> *I am sailing, stormy waters,*
> *To be near you, to be free.*
> —*"Sailing," recorded by Rod Stewart*

When Rod Stewart showed up in the Shoals to work on 1975's *Atlantic Crossing*, he continued what had become a Shoals tradition. Stewart was surprised to learn that the band that backed Aretha Franklin was a bunch of white Alabama boys.

Upon first laying eyes on the rhythm section, Stewart asked his producer, Atlantic's Tom Dowd, to step outside for a talk. Stewart was sure that Dowd had lied to him and that he wouldn't be recording with Aretha Franklin's band, after all.

"It was our goal when we worked with Rod Stewart to sound like Rod Stewart's band and when we worked with Paul Simon to sound like Paul Simon's band," Hood said to the *Birmingham News*'s Bob Carlton.

Hood understood the doubters. "And we looked like—you know, short hair, you know just 'Duh?' you know, guys that worked at the supermarket or something," he later explained to NPR's *Weekend Edition*.

Stewart overcame his skepticism, though, and recorded *Atlantic Crossing*, which firmly established him as a solo artist rather than merely as a member

Rod Stewart's *Atlantic Crossing* symbolized his split from Atlantic Records and also played a role in establishing Stewart as a solo artist rather than just a member of the band Faces. Atlantic Crossing, *Warner Bros., 1975.*

of the British rock band Faces. The single "Sailing" was a United Kingdom hit, although it didn't perform as well in the United States.

Nevertheless, critics recognized this as a new moment in Stewart's career. Of the backing musicians, *Rolling Stone* reviewer Paul Nelson wrote, "The new backup musicians, mainly from Muscle Shoals and Memphis, provide the kind of crisp, authoritative, very spare basics that manage to suggest much of the pre-1975 Stewart as well as something completely different."

> *And sometimes even now, when I'm feeling lonely and beat*
> *I drift back in time and I find my feet*
> *Down on Mainstreet*
> *—"Mainstreet," Bob Seger*

Detroit rock-and-roll musician Bob Seger also found a career turning point in sleepy Sheffield, Alabama.

"If there is any grace in heaven, *Night Moves* will give Bob Seger the national following which has long eluded him," *Rolling Stone* wrote in its review of the 1976 album. "It is simply one of the best albums of the year. As a vocalist, Seger recalls Rod Stewart; his raspy voice can both soar and attack. As a composer, he echoes Bruce Springsteen in his painful attempts to memorialize his past."

The Muscle Shoals Rhythm Section played on about half the album, although Seger's regular Silver Bullet Band received credit on the album's

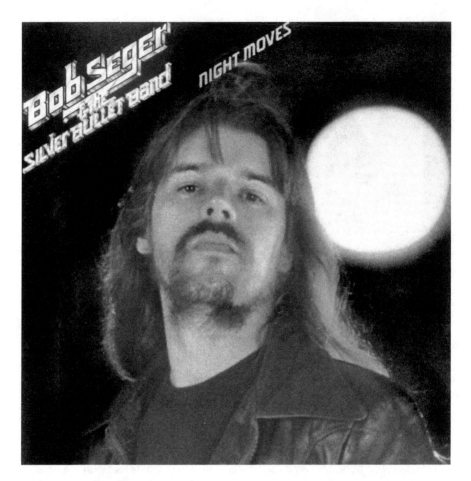

Half of Bob Seger's *Night Moves* was actually recorded with the Muscle Shoals Rhythm Section, although his band the Silver Bullets appears on the album's cover. Night Moves, *Capitol, 1976.*

cover. "Sunspot Baby," "Mainstreet" (which went to number twenty-four on the *Billboard* chart), "Come to Poppa" and "Ship of Fools" were all recorded with the Swampers at Muscle Shoals Sound.

Seger again found success in the Shoals when he returned to cut tracks for his next album, *Stranger in Town*. Sometimes, songs that were intended as demos to be rerecorded later by other artists ended up becoming the backing track for a hit. That was the case when Bob Seger heard the George Jackson– and Thomas Jones III–penned "Old Time Rock and Roll."

Seger attempted to make the song his own, recording it with his band as well as the Swampers. But he couldn't match the energy of the

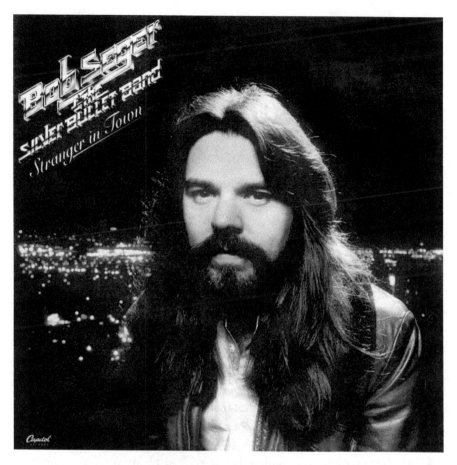

Bob Seger found "Old Time Rock and Roll" on a demo tape from Muscle Shoals Sound and ended up using the original demo music as his backing track. Stranger in Town, *Capitol, 1978.*

original demo—including the "da-da-da-da-da" intro that came from an engineering error. In the end, Seger purchased the demo track and recorded his vocal over it, resulting in the 1979 song that only hit number twenty-eight on the *Billboard* chart but remains a radio favorite today. The band also recorded with him for "We've Got Tonite" (number twelve) and "Katmandu," among others.

12

CONTINUED SUCCESS

I had a woman down in Alabama
She was a backwoods girl, but she sure was realistic
She said, "Boy, without a doubt,
Have to quit your mess and straighten out
You could die down here, be just another accident statistic"
There's a slow, slow train coming up around the bend.
—"Slow Train," Bob Dylan

And the stars kept on coming. In 1978, Bob Dylan arrived in town to record *Slow Train Coming.* By this point, Jerry Wexler and Barry Beckett regularly worked as co-producers. They spent two weeks recording the album with Dylan, and the single "Gotta Serve Somebody" resulted in the songwriter's first Grammy.

"Barry and Dylan hit it off beautifully," Wexler said to *Huntsville Times* reporter John Wessel. And the result was a success.

"It takes only one listening to realize that *Slow Train Coming* (Columbia Records) is the best album Bob Dylan has made since *The Basement Tapes* (recorded with the Band in 1967 but not released until 1975)," Jann Wenner wrote in his *Rolling Stone* review.

Bob Dylan has, at long last, come back into our lives and times, and it is
with the most commercial LP he's ever released. Slow Train Coming *has*
been made with a care and attention to detail that Dylan never gave any

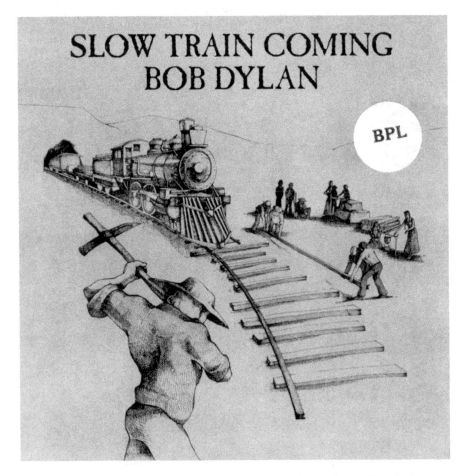

Bob Dylan recorded two "Christian era" albums at Muscle Shoals Sound. Slow Train Coming, *Columbia, 1979.*

of his earlier records. The decision to take such time and care comes from a deep artistic and personal re-evaluation. He wanted—and after so many weak efforts and near failures, perhaps felt he had no choice—a commercial success. He was also smart enough to see that this thrust might even be the only road left for his return to brilliance. The musicians on this album are the best Dylan has worked with since Highway 61 Revisited *(1965),* Blonde on Blonde *(1966) and* The Basement Tapes *(1967).*

Later in the review, Wenner noted that "Gonna Change My Way of Thinking" evoked the Rolling Stones' "Brown Sugar," also recorded with the Swampers.

Bob Dylan's *Saved*, released in 1980, was something of a follow-up to his previous Christian-themed work, *Slow Train Coming*. Saved *(rereleased cover), Columbia, 1990, originally released in 1980.*

"Musically, this is probably Dylan's finest record, a rare coming together of inspiration, desire and talent that completely fuse strength, vision and art."

Kurt Loder, who in 1980 reviewed the second of Dylan's "Christian" albums for *Rolling Stone*, disagreed with Wenner's effusive praise for *Slow Train Coming*. But the latter of the pair of albums earned Loder's respect.

"*Saved* is a much more aesthetically gratifying LP than its predecessor, particularly because of the hope (mostly musical, I admit) it offers that Dylan may eventually rise above the arid confines of Biblical literalism," Loder wrote. "Maybe he'll evolve, maybe he'll just walk away. Whichever the case, stagnation has never been his style, and after *Saved*, there seems precious little left to say about salvation through dogma." He went on to note that the band itself sounded sharper than expected, much more satisfying to the reviewer than the rhythm-and-blues inflection of *Slow Train Coming*.

Success wasn't always a guaranteed outcome, though. In 1982, Wexler returned to Muscle Shoals Sound with singer Lou Ann Barton in tow. He again produced an album with the rhythm section, but the results were more akin to early efforts with Cher and Lulu than the great albums that had come out of the studio. "But the album, *Old Enough*, just wasn't good enough," Wexler wrote in his autobiography.

Ever since you've been far away, I've been wanting to fly.
Now I know what you meant to me, I'm the one who should cry.
And it's much too late for good-byes, yes, it's much too late for good-byes.
—"Too Late for Goodbyes," Julian Lennon

Some musicians could skate by on the strength of their names, either because of earlier work or because of family ties. The latter could have been true for Julian Lennon, son of Beatle John Lennon. But producer Phil Ramone wanted to safeguard his client. So when it came time to record the younger Lennon's debut album, Ramone settled on Muscle Shoals Sound.

"The most important element is the quality of musicians, producers, writers and engineers included with the pleasant Southern surroundings. Work comes first here," a 1984 *TimesDaily* article explained. "But it's not a pressure situation. It's an atmosphere of dedication and excitement in the studios. The locals are knowledgeable of each artist that comes here to record. And down here, time is not something that just flies by."

Lennon seemed to benefit from that atmosphere. The album's title track, "Valotte," hit number nine on the *Billboard* chart, spending twelve weeks total in that vicinity. Two decades later, Lennon remains an active musician.

I'm never gonna dance again
Guilty feet have got no rhythm
Though it's easy to pretend
I know you're not a fool
—"Careless Whisper," George Michael

Although the version of "Careless Whisper" that endures was recorded elsewhere, another, very similar, recording of the song was a Japanese hit.

JULIAN LENNON   VALOTTE

Julian Lennon wrote the title track to *Valotte*, his debut album, while overlooking the river from outside Muscle Shoals Sound Studio's Alabama Avenue location. Valotte, *Charisma, 1984.*

Wexler produced the George Michael song, with vocals recorded in the Shoals and the strings in Nashville. "Our version came out only in Japan, though some think, because of the live fiddles, the American rendition has the edge," Wexler wrote. That rendition held strong at *Billboard*'s number-one position for three weeks and remained on the chart for seventeen weeks total.

Down home blues, down home blues
All I wanna hear is these down home blues
All night long, every other record or two

How the Swampers Changed American Music

Now take off those fast jams
And let me hear some down home blues, alright
—"Down Home Blues," recorded by Etta James

Wexler left the Shoals for seven years, but he returned to the area in 1991, this time to work with Etta James on her album *The Right Time*. He previously worked with James on *Deep in the Night*, recorded at FAME in 1968. "Not only was I working again with one of my favorite singers, but I was also back at the scene of many previous crimes, Muscle Shoals. All the way back home. Both Etta and I were determined to make a quintessential rhythm-and-blues album—no compromises, no nonsense, just righteous and raw," Wexler wrote in *Rhythm and Blues: A Life in American Music*. Steve Winwood joined in on the project, as well, reuniting with the rhythm section that briefly had supported Traffic in the '70s.

"We had to be careful not to make a retro-sounding record," Wexler said to the *Huntsville Times*. "The idea was to use the connection with what I call 'American root music' to be found there, but to bring it up into the '90s. We accomplished it, in my opinion."

Rolling Stone reviewer John Swenson seemed to agree:

> *There is no greater living blues singer than Etta James, and no producer more attuned to the right setting for a blues diva than Jerry Wexler. The recent collaboration between these two giants,* The Right Time, *is as spectacular an update of R&B as that statement suggests it would be. The album is overpowering in its stylistic force. Its material is drawn from an R&B treasure-trove dating back to early Atlantic sides and covering the history of Southern soul from Sixties Stax through Seventies Hi and Eighties Malaco. The result is a sound steeped in tradition but as fresh as a magnetic $100 bill.*

I left Texas with good intentions
Getting back home's been a bone of contention
It sounded like a good idea at the time
But I've run out of reasons and I'm all out of rhyme
I've got to get back to what I like best
I'm headed south by southwest
—"South by Southwest," recorded by Lee Roy Parnell

Nashville songwriter Lee Roy Parnell recorded his first album in the Shoals at age eighteen. He chose to record in the area because so many of

97

the musicians he looked up to had done so in the past—the Allman Brothers Band chief among them. Years later, Parnell returned to Muscle Shoals Sound to record *Tell the Truth*, released on June 12, 2001, by Vanguard Records. Johnny Sandlin produced the record, and Parnell's friends Delbert McClinton—who found success at Muscle Shoals Sound himself with 1980's *The Jealous Kind* and the *Billboard* top-twenty hit "Giving It Up for Your Love"—Bonnie Bramlett, Keb Mo and others joined him on vocals. (The album failed to chart.)

Although the Swampers themselves are the musicians most closely associated with the studio, a number of others have found success starting here and continuing with other projects. Wayne Perkins, who recorded on a number of projects at Muscle Shoals Sound, later toured with Eric Clapton and Leon Russell and recorded with acts including Joni Mitchell, John Prine, Levon Helm and more.

Because Muscle Shoals Sound was, for most of its existence, a tracking studio, not a producing studio, more musicians recorded at 3614 Jackson Highway and later at 1000 Alabama Avenue than anyone could probably count. While at the original Jackson Highway location, the Swampers recorded thirty to forty albums annually, playing as many as three sessions a day and working six days a week. Take, for example, Rock and Roll Hall of Fame Inductee and blues artist Albert King, who recorded his 1971 album *Lovejoy* in the Shoals. "King has a way of putting over R&B/country/folk, and the backing he has on these sides is really with it," Troy, New York music columnist Tom Thomas wrote.

Some of those artists may not have made it to the *Billboard* charts, but their work retained the Muscle Shoals sound.

13

ALABAMA AVENUE

Sitting on a pebble by the river playing guitar
Wond'ring if we're really ever gonna get that far
Do you know there's something wrong?
'Cause I've felt it all along
—"Valotte," Julian Lennon

As musicians continued to flock to Sheffield to record with the Swampers, the group found itself ready to expand operations. But the group was renting the Jackson Highway studio, and the owner wasn't interested in selling. Instead, the Muscle Shoals Rhythm Section relocated its operations in 1978 two miles away to 1000 Alabama Avenue. The former steam-generating plant and Naval Reserve building was perched on the banks of the Tennessee River. (It was allegedly the inspiration for Julian Lennon's "Valotte": "Sitting on a pebble by the river playing guitar.")

"We had more business than we could handle, and there was no place to go. So that's when we moved," David Hood said to *Songfacts*.

The owners brought the Muscle Shoals Sound name with them. The new space offered two studios and twenty-four tracks, rather than the eight-track machines they had previously used. It was a large studio complex under one roof. With the move, the Muscle Shoals Rhythm Section also shifted to producing more albums, rather than cutting original tracks that would often be finished elsewhere.

In 1979, Muscle Shoals Sound Studio needed more space, so it moved to a former steam-generating plant and Naval Reserve building overlooking the Tennessee River. *George F. Landegger Collection of Alabama Photographs in Carol M. Highsmith's America, Library of Congress, Prints and Photographs Division. Gift, George F. Landegger, 2010 (DLC/PP-2010:090).*

Downtown Florence in the 1980s. *Martin Colyer.*

The studio was part of a growing trend: older, "fingerprint" rooms closing in favor of newer facilities or because of other complications. Motown's Hitsville U.S.A. relocated from Detroit to Los Angeles in 1972, and Memphis's Stax Records filed for bankruptcy in 1975.

The legend of Muscle Shoals extends far outside its region, attracting bands from around the world to record in the legendary studio. *Martin Colyer.*

The local recording scene continued to thrive after the move, and Muscle Shoals Sound remained a vital part of the industry. In 1982, a Muscle Shoals Music Association Songwriter's Showcase gave the area's writers a chance to show off their skills. Many were writing country music at the time, while others focused on contemporary Christian music. (Appropriately, Bob Dylan's *Slow Train Coming* and *Saved* were recorded at the studio and then released in 1979 and 1980.)

"It's true that Muscle Shoals writes the songs the world sings," MSMA executive director Bill Jarnigan said at the time.

A three-day seminar in 1980 proved that point, drawing more than six hundred people from around the world to the area for discussions about music industry issues.

The country may have been in a recession, but the state's music industry was comfortable, in part because of lean staffs and rather humble studios. Although major recording labels were cutting their expenses, the Shoals remained an affordable place for the big acts to record. At the time, an album cut at Muscle Shoals Sound ran between $50,000 to $60,000—fairly average for the business, but in a town where travel and amenities were more affordable than most music industry hot spots.

Muscle Shoals Sound Studio relocated to 1000 Alabama Avenue in 1979 and continued to operate there until the founders sold the business to Malaco Recording in 1985. *Martin Colyer.*

However, that small-town charm and isolation were the proverbial double-edged sword. There are a number of reasons why things began to slow at Muscle Shoals Sound. The few amenities—once part of the area's appeal—might have frustrated some musicians. It was difficult to get around (Alabama cities aren't exactly known for their public transit options!). In the end, one of the studio's greatest draws—its remote location—might have been a factor in its demise. Even that's hard to say, though, as FAME continues to produce a number of reputable albums decades later.

And although the studio continued to record country and rock bands, as disco increased in popularity, the demand for the area's soulful rhythm and blues waned. Barry Beckett predicted just that, in fact, in an interview with the *Anniston (AL) Star* years earlier. Disco was on its way in, and Beckett told the *Star*'s Tom Gordon he expected the black and lyrically heavy music that had made Muscle Shoals Sound successful would soon be trumped by "make an ass of yourself type" music.

Also, then as now, changing technology posed a threat to the industry. In 1982, Muscle Shoals Music Association executive director Buddy Draper traveled to Washington, D.C., to show support for legislation that would require manufacturers of blank cassette tapes and recording equipment to

The British band Hot House traveled to the States in 1987 to record at Muscle Shoals Sound Studio. *Martin Colyer.*

Producer Johnny Sandlin sits at one of the main analogue consoles used at the Muscle Shoals Sound. Sandlin, who has produced gold records for the Allman Brothers and other acts, said that while digital recording technology constantly becomes cheaper and more powerful, it hasn't completely replaced vintage '70s equipment. *AL.COM/Landov.*

pay royalties to songwriters, musicians and other copyright holders. It was an amendment to Senate bill 1758, which was designed to protect private citizens with home video recording equipment. MSMA worked to include the audio industry in the amendment. The bill did not make it out of committee during the 1982 legislative session.

By 1985, the Swampers were ready for something different. The studio was set for another expansion, but Barry Beckett wanted to try something new. He headed to Nashville, where he worked as a producer. By that time, Beckett had already co-produced a number of albums with Wexler, including Dire Straits' *Communiqué*, Bob Dylan's *Slow Train Coming* and *Saved* and Carlos Santana's *Havana Moon*.

Business started to drop off around the time of the sale. "That was really when disco came in," Jimmy Johnson said to the *(London) Telegraph*. "We just didn't adapt; it wasn't natural to us."

Tommy Couch, Wolf Stephenson and Stewart Madison, the owners of Malaco Music, approached the Swampers with nearly $1 million, ready to purchase the studio, label and publishing company. Although Beckett left, Malaco retained Roger Hawkins, Johnson and Hood to manage the operation. Malaco's musician roster is, even today, largely composed of blues and gospel musicians—which may have made Muscle Shoals Sound a natural fit.

And so it makes sense that the studio owners followed the Muscle Shoals Rhythm Section's lead, sticking to the session-musician mold that had already proven successful. Under Malaco's ownership, the studio pumped out recordings for a variety of artists under the label Muscle Shoals Records, publishing seven albums over the course of several years. That effort went dormant for a time but was revitalized in 1996 with the release of Men of Standard's self-titled debut album. For a time, the two-studio building continued to churn out projects.

But Malaco, too, saw recording opportunities decline. "When computer and hard-disk recording really got cheap and better at the same time, it just knocked the socks off a lot of studios, [Muscle Shoals] included. It was just a very difficult thing to compete with," Malaco principal Wolf Stephenson said in an interview with *Billboard*.

Besides, Stephenson said in the same interview, he and his business partners were truly after the studio's publishing catalogue. "To be quite

Muscle Shoals musicians, including a horn section, are shown in the studio in the '80s. *Martin Colyer.*

The Shoals in the '80s. *Martin Colyer.*

frank with you," Stephenson told Billboard, "the only reason we bought the studio was, the banks we were dealing with wouldn't loan us the money on the publishing company; they didn't have any idea what it was. It was just a stack of paper to them."

Loan officers weren't the only ones ignorant about the significance of the studio and its publishing catalogue. Although the Muscle Shoals studio recording history had, by this point, spanned more than forty years, even some Shoals-area natives weren't aware of the local scene's influence on American music. Florence-raised Randy Poe didn't fully understand the effect of his hometown until he returned in 1977 to study in the University of North Alabama's commercial music business program.

"When the heart of it was going on, when the incredible stuff was being made, I doubt if 10 people in the city knew," Poe said to the *Huntsville Times.*

"People usually don't know what's going on around here until it's done, and they like it like that," former Alabama Music Hall of Fame curator George Lair explained to the *(Mobile, AL) Press-Register.*

For his part, Poe tried to educate his fellow Alabamians. In 1993, Poe celebrated his home's musical legacy with a Rhino Records compilation, *Muscle Shoals Sound.* The eighteen-track album, which is now out of print, included a variety of hits from the region's history. Early success stories such as Aretha Franklin, Wilson Pickett, Arthur Alexander and Percy Sledge are all represented, as are Muscle Shoals Sound hits, including "Take a Letter, Maria" by R.B. Greaves and the Staple Singers' "I'll Take You There."

But sometimes you don't recognize what you have until it's gone. As the industry continued to shift, the recording portion of Malaco's business became less profitable. And so in 2004, the company listed the studio on eBay for $650,000. The price would have included the building, the property on which it sat and the equipment inside, but the auction site didn't generate offers.

Hood worried about what that could mean for the Muscle Shoals legacy. "I'm seeing this place that I worked so hard, and my partners and I worked so hard, to build going to waste and deteriorating because it's not being used," he said to NPR's *Weekend Edition*. "And my biggest fear is if they don't find a buyer, they're just going to take it, dismantle it and sell it piece at a time. You know, that would break my heart."

After more than a year and a half with the building and equipment on the market, the company was ready to go another route.

In 2005, Tonya S. Holly of Cypress Moon Productions purchased the Alabama Avenue property. Cypress Moon offered for Hood to retain his office in the building, which he maintained throughout the Malaco period as something of a storage facility for his gear, awards and photos. But it wouldn't be the same.

"I am mourning the loss of the studios," Hood said at the time to the *Birmingham News*. "But you've got to move on. The recording business has changed so that you don't need to have a big recording studio like you did in the old days. Technology has changed. It's a computer-based situation."

The Alabama Music Hall of Fame requested every Muscle Shoals Sound–related item Malaco had to be donated to the museum, and *Rolling Stone* reported at the time that some of it could end up in the Rock and Roll Hall of Fame and Museum in Cleveland, Ohio. Hood, however, expected the company to sell off each item, piece by piece. Ultimately, that's what happened. Malaco sold equipment to other studios, and the remainder of the studios' contents were sold off piecemeal.

"We did something special in this little bitty town," Hood said to the *Birmingham News*. "Nobody ever thought we would. That whole building is a trophy, and I'm very proud of it."

14

NOEL WEBSTER

Mockingbird, can't you see?
Little girl's got a hold on me
Like glue
Baby, I'm howlin' for you
—*"Howlin' for You," the Black Keys*

Like so many others before him, music brought Noel Webster to the Shoals. But in Webster's case, it was to perform. Webster, who already owned a studio in nearby Huntsville, Alabama, performed in a number of area venues in the late 1990s. Around 2:00 a.m., after a 1999 gig at Sports Rock Café, Webster was chatting with police officers and asked about area recording studios because he was familiar with the area's recording legacy.

"You can't listen to classic rock radio for an hour and not hear a record that was cut here," he said to the *Oxford American* during a 2011 interview.

The officers seized the chance to show Webster a couple former studios, including the then abandoned original home of Muscle Shoals Sound. "They kicked the door open because it was vacant—it had been for a long time," Webster recalls. After the Swampers moved the studio to 1000 Alabama Avenue, the Jackson Highway building was home to an appliance repair shop and an audio parts retailer before sitting vacant.

Once inside, Webster immediately recognized the work of music producer and recording engineer Tom Dowd, a Rock and Roll Hall of Fame inductee, because of the control room window's angles. Dowd's understanding of

The Muscle Shoals area's Old Railroad bridge is now a walking bridge across the Tennessee River. *George F. Landegger Collection of Alabama Photographs in Carol M. Highsmith's America, Library of Congress, Prints and Photographs Division. Gift, George F. Landegger, 2010 (DLC/PP-2010:090).*

science and physics, gleaned before he entered the music business, informed his work in the studio. Dowd had worked in the Shoals several times during his years with Atlantic. Webster's interest was piqued.

Webster, who was also doing some recording work at the Alabama Avenue location of Muscle Shoals Sound, began placing daily calls to the owner of the building at 3614 Jackson Highway. The owner was initially reluctant to sell, but after Webster made a significant down payment, the building was his. Over the years, he also purchased the surrounding property to prevent any infringing businesses. One thing he didn't have to worry about stepping on his toes, though, was a music venue. "It's kind of ironic that after I bought the building, about a year in, the clubs closed," Webster recalled with a laugh.

The building was in disrepair, but after touring it with a real estate agent friend, Webster realized that its small size meant there wasn't a lot to fix. The roof needed to be repaired and the air-conditioning unit to be replaced, but those seemed surmountable.

For a time, Webster considered outfitting the room with modern-day equipment. Then he tested the room's sound.

"I knew I had to put it back," he said to the *TimesDaily* in a 2001 interview. "There's no other room that sounds like this."

Webster gives a lot of credit to the building's construction. The studio floor is perched on beams and shakes as bands perform on it. "These acoustic spaces are alive and they work with everything, from acoustic guitars to pianos to handclaps to singing," Webster said to the *Oxford American*. That was true in Wexler's day, he said, and remains so.

And so Webster filled the space with vintage equipment, evocative of the studio's heyday. He wanted to re-create the sound that made Muscle Shoals legendary—and perhaps the kind of chart-climbing hits that accompanied it.

"At every stage, we'd treat it like an archaeological dig," Webster recalled. "[We] didn't tear out anything that didn't need torn out." The building's status as a national historic site, achieved during Webster's ownership, required certain cautionary measures; repairs had to preserve the building's original appearance, although Webster and his crew were able to add a staircase next to the bathroom because it was an unphotographed area.

"We tried to save everything we could," he said in a 2005 interview with the *TimesDaily*. "It's still a working studio."

Guitars and amplifiers hearkened to the 1970s, when the studio called the Jackson Highway building home. Some of the equipment Webster incorporated also came from well-known musicians. For example, Ted Nugent donated his Mesa Boogie amplifiers, and Bobby Whitlock, who played with such acts as Derek and the Dominoes ("Layla," "Bell Bottom Blues") and George Harrison ("All Things Must Pass"), offered his keyboard to the studio. While the stories that accompanied each piece were special, these were also functioning musical instruments and equipment.

Swampers Jimmy Johnson and David Hood periodically visited during the building's restoration to ensure that Webster's re-creation was an accurate reflection of their work. According to the application filed to the National Register of Historic Places, which references a 2001 *TimesDaily* article, Johnson said, "Noel is really doing it right. Not only can he keep the old thing alive, he can do a lot of sessions from all over the world."

However, for a time Webster lived in the building's basement—certainly not a callback to the studio's most productive hours, although surely many musicians spent long hours in the building. Even so, he filled the rooms with music memorabilia, including a tape machine that he said once belonged to John Lennon and set lists from Rolling Stones performances.

By 2001, Muscle Shoals Sound Studio was back in business.

On April 1 of that year, a team of studio musicians gathered at 3614 Jackson Highway for the first recording session during Webster's ownership. It wasn't until later that the group realized that the thirteen-hour Sunday recording session also marked thirty-two years to the day since the studio opened.

That 2001 Tommy York and Thrillbilly project marked the first of many to be recorded in the studio's newest era. Webster saw a number of bands come through during his time as owner of Muscle Shoals Sound, none more prominent than rock duo the Black Keys, who recorded there in 2009.

As bands came through, they often recorded songs live, with each musician and his or her equipment in the same room. Although some studios isolate each instrument or vocal from the others for technical reasons, Webster believed that playing through songs as a band helped to capture the energy on tape. He engineered albums and handled the mastering, as well.

"The bleed-through is what made the album," guitarist Jason Humphress of King's Haze explained to the *Huntsville Times*. Humphress and his Huntsville-based band recorded with Webster in 2012.

The recordings weren't the only hallmark of the Webster era. In 2006, the building received National Register of Historic Places status, thanks to the application filed by Gene Ford in the University of Alabama's Office of Archeological Research.

But Webster's time in the Shoals lasted little more than a decade. The Black Keys' 2010 Grammy Award–winning album *Brothers* brought widespread attention, both good and bad, back to the Shoals sound for the first time in decades. Soon after, Greg "Freddy" Camalier came to town and filmed the documentary *Muscle Shoals*, which generated even more interest in the area's legendary sound.

Meanwhile, a buddy of Webster's asked why he ever left Huntsville. "When we were playing at your studio in Huntsville way back when, I always liked that room in Huntsville. It sounded great there. Why did you go out there? Why not come back home?" Webster recalled musician Jim Parker asking. "Why not just do that and just own a house and be done with it and put my studio there? So that's what I did."

In 2013, Webster put the building on the market, and he said he quickly received a variety of offers. But Muscle Shoals Music Foundation was the natural buyer. The movie had generated so much interest in the area that the local music and tourism scenes seemed poised to do something big. But without the original Muscle Shoals Sound in the arsenal, drawing attention to town would be difficult.

The foundation acquired the building in June of that year.

"I think it's fantastic. Somebody had to save it," Webster said. "When I bought it, they literally had the cranes out. The city told me, 'You've got 90 days to bring this up to code or we're going to mow it down.' The mayor told me, 'We're going to tear that whole block down because it's condemned.'" Now, the studio's ownership has transferred into new hands to carry the legacy forward.

15

THE BLACK KEYS

Let me be your everlasting light
Your sun when there is none
I'm a shepherd for you
And I'll guide you through
Let me be your everlasting light
—*"Everlasting Light," the Black Keys*

Rock duo the Black Keys already had five albums under its belt, including Danger Mouse–produced *Attack & Release*, before it turned its attention to Muscle Shoals. Although the two had seen some success, including Canadian gold-album status for *Attack & Release*, *Brothers* marked the start of something new for the pair.

Drummer Patrick Carney and singer/guitarist Dan Auerbach connected with producer and engineer Mark Neill early in the process of recording their sixth studio album. Neill was reputed to create records with a distinctive sound, in part because of his affection for vintage equipment. The Georgia-raised professional spent much of the '80s building his collection of such and has worked with bands such as the Old '97s.

"Dan liked what he'd heard on some of my records and asked if he could come by for a visit," Neill said to *Sound on Sound*. He wasn't terribly familiar with the Black Keys' music, but Neill said he quickly understood that Auerbach was deeply interested in the process of making albums like Neill's.

The Black Keys' 2010 Grammy Award–winning *Brothers* was one of the first recordings made at Muscle Shoals Sound in decades. Brothers, *Nonesuch, 2010.*

Neill was engineer and mixer for Auerbach's *Keep It Hid*, his 2009 solo debut. Auerbach later returned to Neill's La Mesa, California home with Carney. Together, they began recording "These Days," which eventually became the final track on the band's 2010 effort *Brothers*.

Ultimately, Neill would later say, the band wanted to record somewhere outside the norm, and it wanted the resulting album to reflect a swampy southern sound.

But options were limited: Memphis's Sun Records' Sam C. Phillips was booked, and Sun's original studio conducted tours during the day and only allowed nighttime recordings. Muscle Shoals Sound was not the studio it once was, but Neill and the Black Keys decided to head for

Alabama. Auerbach suggested the trio haul in the necessary equipment to make it work.

"I mean, I love the sound of those old Muscle Shoals records," Neill said to *Sound on Sound*, "but I can't say that it was actually my idea to go there. But hey, as long as there was air conditioning and reliable electricity, I was willing."

"Muscle Shoals isn't the holy grail," Auerbach said to *Soma* magazine. "No matter where we made this record, we were going to hunker down and focus, but I'm into the old recording studios from the late '50s and early '60s. That was the golden age of music production, when they recorded live bands playing together in one room."

A call to Noel Webster confirmed that Neill's must-haves would be met, but not much else. "Noel was a nice enough guy who was willing to cut the Black Keys a really good day rate, albeit with the clear understanding that we were getting nothing but an empty building with a bathroom, and yes, air conditioning. So we knew right from the start that we really would be trucking in our own equipment," Neill said.

And so the planning began. Neill devised a plan for carting his equipment two thousand miles away and established expectations for the sessions. He later said five backing tracks—no vocals—would have been a success, given the circumstances.

A contingency plan was also a must. Since the studio hadn't been operating at its original capacity for three decades, Neill wasn't sure what to expect from the power. If an electrical surge blew something, he knew he could drive to Nashville for replacement parts. Finally, Neill conducted a run-through before hitting the road, testing to be sure every possible hurdle had been eliminated.

The only obstacle that remained before Neill, Auerbach and Carney could discover whether the Muscle Shoals sound was still thriving was a drive to Alabama.

"We already had the material from my studio, so if the worst came to the worst, we could have always just headed back there and finished the record, or gone up to Dan's place in Akron," Neill said to *Sound on Sound*. "At the very least, anything we did in Alabama could have been used as demos—albeit expensive ones."

August 16, 2009, marked forty years since R.B. Greaves recorded the studio's first hit. It was also the day the band and Neill arrived in the Shoals, a truckload of gear in tow and two weeks of studio time booked. As had been the norm in the '70s, the band focused on the music in part because there wasn't much else to do. The Black Keys recorded ten of *Brothers*'s fifteen tracks quickly.

The assembled team worked to replicate the magic of the studio's heyday. "We just used the same techniques that they used in the '50s and '60s and '70s, and that's what seems to work," Webster said to *SongFacts*. "Our equipment is hot-rodded a little bit, so it's not like you can go out and buy a piece of equipment that's in this building and use it somewhere else. It's modified, put it that way."

Webster had tried to restore the room's sound, placing the studio's original consoles back in their previous homes and duplicating the audio path that existed.

Neill quickly realized how the room had affected the classic Muscle Shoals Sound recordings he so loved. The building's acoustics were a major factor.

"The control room has this real mid-range 'bark,' and as a result you tend to mix things a certain way. So much so that when you go out to the car or listen through your ear buds back at the hotel, you suddenly realize, 'Jeez, I've done this completely differently,'" he explained to *Sound on Sound* a year after the album's release.

Muscle Shoals Sound recordings tend to have prominent kick drum and bass for that reason. The floors have a lot of flex in them, though, which makes them emulate a bass trap.

"In this case, we were going for a fuzzed sound when it felt right," Neill added—a sound that again recalled some of the studio's best-known work. Overdriving the console, whether intentionally (as it was in Neill's case) or not, created that vibe.

The recording method for *Brothers* was also something of a throwback. Most modern records utilize a number of audio tracks, which can make mixing complex. But for *Brothers*, the band used four microphones and focused on making decisions in the moment rather than in the post-recording process.

"I know there are some people who think the whole thing was overblown, that the studio had nothing to do with it. And to some degree, they're right—the songs on *Brothers* are incredible, and maybe they would have come out just as well under different circumstances," Neill said to *Sound on Sound*. "Still, having the opportunity to cut that music in that studio was something I'll never forget. I got to witness first hand that it really isn't folklore—that those guys back then knew exactly what they were doing when they built that place. It was a room that was really intelligently designed, and nothing in there happened by accident. And that even after all this time, there still can be a Muscle Shoals sound."

Although the area's dearth of entertainment options was part of what drew bands to it to begin with, after ten days and recording ten songs, the Black Keys were restless. Their time in the Shoals was over.

"Here we are walking around with a bag of Funyuns, totally burned out," Auerbach said to *Rolling Stone*, which described the album as darker than their previous effort, *Attack & Release*.

The band later cleaned up the signature Muscle Shoals swampy sound with modern technology. The remaining soul-inflected vibe came more from the music the band was into at the time (lots of soul and hip-hop), not from the studio, Auerbach said to the *(London) Independent*. The pair also grew up listening to a variety of music from the '60s and '70s, and Auerbach has said he taught himself guitar while listening to and playing along with Sam Cooke records.

When interviewed by the *Independent* about their time at the legendary studio, Carney and Auerbach were cynical at best.

"It didn't have any of the equipment in it that it used to have," Auerbach said. "All of the sound treatment had been ripped out. It used to be all carpeted floors and burlap walls, alcoves for the amplifiers."

In the same article, Carney blamed Neill for the experience. "What happened is we hired this engineer who knows his stuff but is nuts and has a bad attitude. So because he had a problem with the guy at Sam Phillips he told us it was broken, when it wasn't. Every break we get, he's trying to buy the studio, or steal shit off the guy who owns it. He was trying to tell us how to make a record."

Auerbach and Carney discounted the magic—real or perceived—of the Shoals in other interviews, as well.

"I think what we found out, honestly, is that Pat and I can really do it anywhere," Auerbach said to the *(Florence, AL) TimesDaily*. "We can create music anywhere. What we learned about Muscle Shoals Sound Studio, and probably all the old studios for that part, is that it's not about that room. It's about those musicians, and the engineers that recorded them. That's what makes the sound."

But their producer said otherwise. Neill told *Sound on Sound*, "Things were happening that were very, very transcendent, as soon as they began playing. First few takes, we literally couldn't believe what we were hearing. Dan and Pat were kind of looking at each other saying, 'That doesn't even sound like us.' Seriously."

Although the band's comments rubbed some Shoals residents wrong, Muscle Shoals Music Foundation chair Rodney Hall remains a fan. "Our goal is to get them back down here. I think they've got it going on," he said. "And they said, that proves to me that they can record a hit record anywhere. And in some ways he's right. They had to bring all the old equipment in. They're basically just using the room. They could've recorded in a garage somewhere."

Whatever the case, the album was an undeniable success. *Rolling Stone* gave it four stars out of five. Critic David Fricke noted, "On *Brothers*, their first studio album after a year of offshoot affairs (Auerbach's solo album, *Keep It Hid*; Carney's side group, Drummer; a hip-hop project, BlakRoc), the Keys make a thick, dirty racket, overdubbed but never overstuffed...*Brothers*, recorded largely in Muscle Shoals, Alabama, with little outside help, has a higher ratio of compelling songs and distress [than 2008's *Attack & Release*]."

Brothers went gold and won three Grammy awards, including Best Alternative Music Album, Best Rock Performance by a Duo or Group (for "Tighten Up," which Danger Mouse produced) and Best Recording Package for the Michael Carney–designed packaging.

It was the first hit album recorded at 3614 Jackson Highway in three decades.

16

A MEMORIAL TO MUSIC

Another day another letter
Would bring me closer to your side
Another walk along the river
Another need be satisfied
—"Another Day (Another Letter)," Boz Scaggs

Even as it rose to prominence, for decades there wasn't an official museum to celebrate and document Alabama's musical history. Muscle Shoals Sound Studio had been operated as something of a museum during Noel Webster's tenure as owner, and the Muscle Shoals City Hall has exhibited a small collection of paraphernalia related to the city's music industry.

The area features a few music attractions, but they're limited. History is on display at the Alabama Music Hall of Fame. FAME Recording Studios and Muscle Shoals Sound Studio are open regularly for tours; Cypress Moon Productions, which now occupies Muscle Shoals Sound's former Alabama Avenue location, allows visitors to tour its facility by appointment; and Father of the Blues W.C. Handy's birthplace serves as a museum just outside downtown Florence.

The Alabama Music Hall of Fame's history is closely tied to Muscle Shoals. Bobby Denton, who recorded one of the first homegrown hits, "A Fallen Star," in 1957, went on to become a state senator. In 1980, he had a hand in legislation that would develop the hall of fame, which celebrates not only the

The Muscle Shoals Music Association, an organization of recording studio owners, producers, musicians, songwriters and other music professionals, created the Alabama Music Hall of Fame Board in 1980 with a mandate to honor all of this state's great music achievers and build a facility to showcase their talent. *George F. Landegger Collection of Alabama Photographs in Carol M. Highsmith's America, Library of Congress, Prints and Photographs Division. Gift, George F. Landegger, 2010 (DLC/PP-2010:090).*

Hits by Alabama musicians play as visitors tour the Alabama Music Hall of Fame. *George F. Landegger Collection of Alabama Photographs in Carol M. Highsmith's America, Library of Congress, Prints and Photographs Division. Gift, George F. Landegger, 2010 (DLC/PP-2010:090).*

Above: Guests to the Alabama Music Hall of Fame can walk through an oversized jukebox while listening to the state's musical hits. *George F. Landegger Collection of Alabama Photographs in Carol M. Highsmith's America, Library of Congress, Prints and Photographs Division. Gift, George F. Landegger, 2010 (DLC/PP-2010:090).*

Right: Mississippians have long found musical success in Alabama, just as Alabamians have found their voices in Mississippi. This sign outside the Alabama Music Hall of Fame commemorates the relationship between the two. *Author's collection.*

THE BLUES TRAIL: MISSISSIPPI TO ALABAMA

Musicians have long crossed the Alabama-Mississippi border to perform and record. Mississippians such as Albert King, Little Milton, and Pops Staples recorded at studios in Muscle Shoals and Sheffield, including those owned by Mississippi natives Rick Hall and Quin Ivy. Alabamians Jerry "Boogie" McCain, Frederick Knight and Roscoe Robinson recorded for labels in Jackson, Mississippi, while Florence native W. C. Handy encountered the blues while working in the Mississippi Delta.

MISSISSIPPI BLUES COMMISSION

legendary "Muscle Shoals Sound" but also the Alabama artists who have changed the landscape of other genres and in other states.

That notion moved from dream to reality in the '80s. The hall of fame hosted its first banquet in 1985. The state approved construction in 1987, Tuscumbia donated the land and organizers broke ground on June 1, 1989. The hall of fame opened barely more than a year later, on July 26, 1990.

Much like other Shoals-area landmarks, the museum is unimpressive from the outside but offers insight into decades of music. As visitors walk through the exhibits, they can read about a variety of musicians while listening to some of the state's most famous songs playing overhead. A tour bus that belonged to the band Alabama invites guests in, and the Muscle Shoals portion includes a working recording studio.

In sum, the museum includes more than four hundred pieces of Alabama music paraphernalia worth $1.4 million (according to insurance assessments). But because the exhibits are static, critics note that visitors are unlikely to return after they've seen it once.

Shoals-related Alabama Music Hall of Fame inductees include W.C. Handy (1987), Sam Phillips (1987), Jerry Wexler (1987, the first nonnative inductee), Muscle Shoals Rhythm Section (1987, contemporary achievement awards), Clarence Carter (1989, contemporary achievement awards), Dan Penn (1991, contemporary achievement awards) and Spooner Oldham (1991, contemporary achievement awards), among others. Though the band hailed from Jacksonville, Florida, Lynyrd Skynyrd received the Alabama Music Heritage Award in 2001.

The Muscle Shoals Rhythm Section was inducted into the Alabama Music Hall of Fame in 1995 (lifework award). The group appeared on a total of more than five hundred recordings, more than seventy-five of which hit gold or platinum. They are also members of the Nashville-based Musicians Hall of Fame, into which they were inducted in 2008.

Dick Cooper, who left journalism and worked for years as Swamper Barry Beckett's production assistant, created many of the museum's exhibits. His work has also been displayed elsewhere. His photograph of Jerry Wexler and Willie Nelson, taken outside the 3614 Jackson Highway studio, was included in the Smithsonian's 150th anniversary exhibit in 1996, and the image also appears on the dust cover of Wexler's autobiography, *Rhythm & the Blues: A Life in American Music.*

Despite the musical legacy of the area in which it resides, the museum's history has been bumpy. It closed for a time in late 2012 through 2013 because funding had dried up. The hall of fame was cut from the state's general fund

The Muscle Shoals Rhythm Section exhibit at Alabama Music Hall of Fame. *Author's collection.*

budget in 2011—which the Alabama Tourism Department had deemed the Year of Alabama Music. During the course of the museum's thirty-year funding, which predates construction, the state had contributed nearly $6.25 million, with as much as $407,000 being distributed to the museum in a single year. The museum shuttered from March 21, 2012, to June 14, 2012. The Northwest-Shoals Community College helped reopen it, but later that year, the school's bid to buy the museum collapsed. It closed again in December 2012 and remained closed until October 17, 2013.

"We find it extremely ironic that the Muscle Shoals sound, starting with the (documentary) premiere at the Sundance film festival, will be celebrated worldwide over the next couple years, while our home state can't find a few hundred thousand dollars out of a $1,769,000,000 budget to honor the single biggest positive image of our state worldwide," Alabama Music Hall of Fame board member and FAME Recording Studios president Rodney Hall said to the *TimesDaily* during the museum's closure. "That's a 1.7 billion general fund. Alabama music: zero."

Even so, Hall has admitted a number of times that the museum has yet to reach its potential. That could influence its future success.

"Our area and our state haven't embraced it," Hall said to the *TimesDaily*. "Look at what Mississippi has done with their music and what Tennessee has done with theirs."

"I don't think we ever got the vision that Alabama music is a huge brand, and Muscle Shoals music specifically a huge brand," Hall said. "We've never attached a star to it and taken advantage of it. I think that's starting to change."

During 2013, the museum's debt had reached $120,000, while news reports suggested its coffers held less than $1,000. Hall indicated that at best one-third of the museum's budget was funded by the income it generates; everything else came from the state. The museum has reported visitor numbers as high as 33,532 in 2007, but only 15,267 guests were recorded in 2010. According to a *New York Times* article, that total dropped to about 12,500 in 2012. Those ticket sales would account for one-third of the museum's operating costs.

As the debate surrounding the museum's closure burned bright, the local paper weighed in with solutions. "The best hope may be in narrowing the hall of fame's focus to the Shoals' rich music scene," said an editorial in the *TimesDaily*. "People from around the world know about the Muscle Shoals sound, but if they visit here there isn't much to see other than historical markers and private recording studios."

"There's a lot of passer-by traffic, but not a lot of traffic that will stop. The No. 1 rule in retail is location, location, location. That's one we missed out on," Hall said to the *New York Times*.

The museum's board likewise suggested a number of options for the hall of fame's future. It could be consolidated with a state welcome center, although the Mississippi state line is a thirty-minute drive away. The idea would have required state funding for at least four years. The board also considered spreading the museum's memorabilia throughout the state so that it could be enjoyed far and wide. After all, attractions such as Huntsville's U.S. Space and Rocket Center are located just off the interstate and attract significantly more visitors than the museum.

"I have always advocated involving the whole state and giving other areas of Alabama a sense of ownership in the hall of fame," former curator George Lair said to the *TimesDaily*. "You will get new and more creative ideas if other areas of the state are involved."

Another option was to keep the museum in Tuscumbia. Data shows that 23,600 cars pass the current location daily, which means a number of potential visitors already exist on the high-traffic route. "We've never seen what it could be with a good marketing plan," former state senator Bobby Denton said to the *TimesDaily.*

The board also issued a call for proposals from cities that would like to relocate the museum. But on October 17—which Alabama governor Robert J. Bentley declared "Muscle Shoals Music Day"—the museum reopened. In a proclamation decreeing the day's observance, Bentley noted the area's music industry dating back to the 1950s.

But that history is far from complete. Curator Cooper said the museum's success will depend in part on the success of the *Muscle Shoals* documentary. Within months after its reopening, the facility was again seeing one thousand visitors per month.

From 1969 to 1978, Muscle Shoals Sound drew a number of artists to Sheffield. Although the hall of fame has seen troubled times, there are still reasons to believe that renewed interest in the area's legacy could revive its tourism appeal.

17

DOCUMENTING THE SOUND

Hmm, when my life is over and my time has run out
My friends and my loved ones
I'll leave there ain't no doubt
But one thing's for certain
When it comes my time
I'll leave this old world with a satisfied mind.
—*"A Satisfied Mind," Bob Dylan*

Who would have thought that a guy from Colorado would bring the Shoals back into the limelight? But then again, who would have expected so much of the Muscle Shoals story to unfold as it did?

In the 2010s, Greg "Freddy" Camalier agreed to keep a friend company on a road trip that ended with the friend's relocation to New Mexico. As they drove through Alabama, the friends realized they were forty miles outside Muscle Shoals. They recognized the area as the place where some of their favorite music was recorded, and so they pulled a U-turn and headed back into town.

If they hadn't, there's no telling where the Shoals music scene would be today.

"We both knew some of the music that we loved all our lives was from there but had no idea of the magnitude," Camalier said to *Rolling Stone*.

The area captured Camalier's heart, and he felt there was a story to be told. And so he set to work directing the documentary film *Muscle Shoals*, which debuted in 2013 at Sundance Film Festival.

The film may be best described as the Muscle Shoals story through the lens of Rick Hall. Camalier, a first-time filmmaker, and his crew incorporated the stories of both FAME and Muscle Shoals Sound, but Hall is the heart of the story.

"If it was just about the music, it would be 12 hours long. This is a story about uniquely talented people and how they worked together," Camalier said to *Billboard.*

The film includes interviews with many of the key players in forming the Muscle Shoals Sound: Hall himself, as well as his son Rodney, who is now president of the Muscle Shoals Music Foundation and of FAME itself; Roger Hawkins, Jimmy Johnson and David Hood of the Muscle Shoals Rhythm Section (Barry Beckett died in 2009); the legendary FAME writing team of Dan Penn and Spooner Oldham; musicians who recorded in the area, including Aretha Franklin, Candi Staton, Mick Jagger and Keith Richards; artists from the Shoals, such as John Paul White of the Civil Wars; and musicians who could speak to the area's influence, including Bono and Alicia Keys.

"It's the most soulful American history lesson I've ever had," musician David MacKay said to the *TimesDaily* after the film's debut. "It's not about facts—it's about the hearts and souls of the people. To listen to this, it just speaks to who dug the well we're all drinking from today. It was very humbling."

Rick Hall is the hero of the movie, easily, with the Swampers' story providing a secondary narrative thread.

"One of [the] things we had going for us was the story itself, which is a huge American music roots story, and musicians know about this story. And a lot of those guys are very willing and sort of honored to shed light into that, and that musicians that came before that—especially musicians who never had their day in the sun," Camalier said to Alabama news site AL.com. "So they sort of came out in the service of the story of Muscle Shoals, which needed to be told."

The film also touched on the unusual way black and white people worked together in the studio. Camalier was surprised that, although the area was in its heyday during and after the civil rights movement, integration was the norm in the studio.

"This colorblind recording history is fascinating. Several people in the film reminisce about how pioneering Hall was in his championing of black musicians, in both a place and a time in which segregation was still the norm," the *Washington Post* noted in its three-and-a-half star review.

Despite all the changes in personnel over the years the number of studio musicians that have made their living in Muscle Shoals is probably still under 100. And there was an effort not to develop a distinctive style. The effort was to become the band of the artist on the studio floor at that time.
—Alabama Music Hall of Fame curator Dick Cooper to swampland.com.

The result is a 111-minute, artistic depiction of the area's musical history, combined with a soundtrack that highlights some of the best of the Muscle Shoals sound and gorgeous views of the surrounding landscape. And the film almost immediately generated buzz; the premiere was sold out, with lines of people waiting to get in. The filmmakers later showed their work around the country, often at special events such as South by Southwest music and technology festival in Austin, Texas, and the Florence premiere, where many of the area's musicians and other key cultural figures gathered.

Reviews were mixed; some critics, such as the *(Newark, NJ) Star-Ledger*'s Stephen Whitty, wrote that the film focused too much on pretty scenes and unnecessary moments. An Alicia Keys recording session, for example, could have been discarded in service of the story. The *Washington Post* noted in its review that Bono comes across as the "resident expert," although he has not recorded in the area.

"The documentary is a little slapdash, but then so is the very idea of what Muscle Shoals means. Is it the town itself? Or the celebrated rhythm section that started at one studio and then formed its own?" Whitty wrote. "Actually, it's both. But mostly it's a sound."

The film's success was recognized in other ways. It was the story of the year for the local paper, the *TimesDaily*, and earned a 96 percent approval rating from all reviews collected by the website Rotten Tomatoes. (The same site listed an 88 percent audience rating.)

"I was wiping tears from my eyes tonight," Jimmy Johnson said to the *TimesDaily* following the local premiere. "I would say it was as accurate as I'd ever want. It can't be perfect. In this type of situation, there are different points of view. People saw things differently."

The attention the film generated refocused the spotlight on the northwest Alabama recording industry. State tourism director Lee Sentell noted that it also resulted in reflected glory for the rest of the state's musicians. The owner of Sheffield-based NuttHouse Recording Studio Jimmy Nutt predicted the spotlight created by the film would help bring deserved attention to other area musicians.

The film also had financial benefits; its Florence-area premiere helped raise money for the Southern Music Foundation (later renamed Muscle Shoals Music Foundation), which helped pay off some of the Alabama Music Hall of Fame's debt and began working toward development of a Muscle Shoals–specific exhibit. Alabama Music Hall of Fame executive director Wiley Barnard formed the nonprofit to promote and preserve the history of southern music.

"It's going to do more for Muscle Shoals music and tourism in the area than anything that's happened since the Wilson Dam," FAME Music Publishing president Rodney Hall said of the movie to the *TimesDaily*.

"Only time will tell, but I think there will be a renaissance, and I think more music will continue to come out of there," Camalier said to AL.com in February 2013. In a matter of months, his words would be proven prescient.

18

MARCHING TO A NEW BEAT

Well, we got ups, we got downs,
We got just so high till the sun goes down.
Got the ego, can be abused;
I got my two-toned shoes,
And I can sing the blues.
—*"All in the Name of Rock & Roll," Rod Stewart*

E ven as the documentary reignited passion about the Muscle Shoals Sound, on June 20, 2013, the Muscle Shoals Music Foundation purchased 3614 Jackson Highway from Noel Webster. Thanks to gifts of $75,000 each from two benefactors, combined with the group's fundraising efforts, the foundation became the building's new owner.

"It's going to be a matter now of finding people to help us put it all together. Everybody seems to be excited about trying to save and renovate this building to make it something that will definitely be an asset to the Shoals," foundation chairman Rodney Hall said to the *Huntsville Times* on the occasion of the sale.

There was still a long road to walk, though, to raise funds for the building's restoration.

On November 26, fundraising ceased to be a concern.

Beats Electronics, an audio company formed by artist/producer Dr. Dre and Interscope Geffen A&M chairman Jimmy Iovine, stepped forward to renovate the studio. The company announced its intent to work with

This vintage Muscle Shoals design depicts the 1000 Alabama Avenue studio. *Martin Colyer.*

the foundation to install both modern and vintage gear in 3614 Jackson Highway, creating a hands-on recording lab for students. The company also intends to upgrade FAME Studios. The project caught the company executives' attention in part because of the documentary.

"Jimmy Iovine had been looking for a project like this, to rescue a studio, for a while. They saw the movie and said, 'There it is boys,'" Hall explained to the *TimesDaily.*

About thirty days prior to the announcement, Hall received a message from Rafferty Jackson at Beats, indicating she wanted to discuss the studio project. "I'm thinking this is some regional sales person or whatever," Hall said. "I call, and it's general counsel/VP of the company."

Jackson explained the company's interest in renovating the studio so it could become a working and teaching space for musicians. But there was a catch: The deal needed to be completed quickly, in part so the company could make the announcement in advance of the Christmas shopping season. (A percentage of all sales during the 2013 holiday season benefited the project.)

"I got to get all the Swampers to agree to this. FAME's involved, so I got to get my dad to agree to this. My dad's a guy who wants to send everything to a lawyer," Hall said. "I got it done somehow, some way."

"Magic is a word that's too often misused in the record industry. Muscle Shoals is different, it's one of the rare places where it really exists," Iovine said in a press release. "Anytime you can capture such a distinct and authentic sound over and over again, that's something worth protecting."

Iovine elaborated in an interview with the Associated Press: "It's not as much about the building. It's the aesthetic and the culture we're trying to maintain. It's being passed down. That's why it's so good to have these places around the world because it's a tribal thing, there's a culture being passed down."

Company president Luke Wood in the same story noted that the end result would be more than a memorial to what had come before. "It's a restoration project, but we don't want it to be a museum," Wood said. "We want it to be a living, breathing place where magic can happen again."

The music industry as a whole had for years been struggling to keep up with digital technology and the way that democratized the industry. Classic rooms like Muscle Shoals had been fading away; recall, after all, that the lack of availability at other such spaces was part of why the Black Keys recorded *Brothers* in Sheffield.

Beats's announced plan includes opportunities for aspiring music industry professionals to work at no cost alongside experienced folks, learning in the process, as part of its Sustain the Sound program.

"We want to look back at another Muscle Shoals revival based on what was learned in these studios in the next five to 10 years," Wood said to the Associated Press.

There are so many amazing recordings that came from this area. That makes the local musicians feel like there are pretty big shoes to fill. I think that pushes everyone to try a little harder.
—Louisa Murray of band the Bear to the (University of Alabama)
Crimson White

Beats has a five-year lease on the studio, with the foundation retaining property ownership. The only costs the foundation is expected to incur

Today, Muscle Shoals Sound Studio retains its original logo. *Author's collection.*

during the course of renovation are related to general building maintenance fees, such as taxes and insurance.

"It was in terrible shape when Noel bought it," Hall said to the *Huntsville Times.* "He should be commended for keeping it alive. It would've been torn down by now if it weren't for him."

The infusion of resources and press coverage fit neatly in line with the Muscle Shoals Music Foundation's existing goals.

"They will do it 10 times faster and 10 times better than we would have done it," Hall said to the *TimesDaily.* "We would have had to nickel and dime it."

The foundation's members had planned for a multiphase approach to renovating the space. According to the group's crowd-funding page on volumebee.com, the plan was to raise the money to acquire the building and restore it to emulate the recording conditions during the studio's heyday while also implementing modern technology. Then, the group expected to partner with FAME Studios and the Muscle Shoals Sound Alabama Avenue location, now home to Cypress Moon Productions, to create a tour package in which visitors could see three historic studios in a single trip. Finally, the foundation aimed to raise money to build a Muscle Shoals music museum. That facility could highlight the local industry as well as those who recorded in the area, and Hall explained to the *TimesDaily* that revenue from museum admission, merchandise sales, studio rental and renting the space as an event venue would keep the venture afloat.

"It's really time now for the whole area to start realizing and recognizing its musical heritage," Big River Broadcasting owner Jerry Phillips, son of the legendary recording executive Sam Phillips, said to the *TimesDaily*.

One weekend the foundation planned to open the studio because the Beats folks, movie folks and others were in town for the Alabama Music Hall of Fame induction ceremony. Those folks hadn't been through the Jackson Highway studio before. The foundation decided to go ahead and let the public come through, too, as an afterthought.

Seven hundred people came through that weekend.

The foundation's publicist, Bonnie Bak, was nervous people would think it was a big grand opening, but there was no mistake. "There are so many people who want to see it that we decided to have it open every weekend we could until they [Beats] begin construction," she said. In the first ten weekends, 2,500 guests came, not only from the surrounding area but also from six or seven countries.

"Most of them have such a connection in a real way to the studio," Bak said in an interview with AL.com. "They either worked there, have lived here their whole life or they just have this connection with the music. They want to come see all of it."

And that's not the extent of the visitors, either. Bak frequently visits the studio during the week, and if people want to pop in to see it, she'll let them through the doors. "Every time I'm over there, people come by," she said.

"[Without Beats] we would still be trying to raise money to do anything," Hall said. "But I will say this: Beats or no Beats, we're open on the weekends now over there for tours, and we've sold $60,000 worth of T-shirts in three, four months."

It's helping the foundation, which is able to shift its focus to raising money for other parts of its multiphase plan. Bak said fundraising efforts will increase around the time Beats unveils the renovations. Foundation memberships also contribute.

This isn't the first time a group has tried to resurrect 3614. Webster himself had intended to do so. Before him, Jamie Copeland, a former disc jockey at an area radio station, purchased the building (then an appliance repair shop) with similar dreams in mind.

"If people want to cut a demo and cut it in the same place the Rolling Stones recorded 'Brown Sugar,' this is the only place you can do it," Copeland explained to the *Birmingham News* in 1999.

HOW THE SWAMPERS CHANGED AMERICAN MUSIC

With the Beats project, David Hood and Jimmy Johnson have been able to meet with architects and tech people. "We're in real accord with what they want to do," Johnson said. Plans include some of the best equipment on the market, even better in some cases than what the Muscle Shoals Rhythm Section had in the original studio. Hall said Beats is also working to find some of the original equipment and instruments, and renowned audio designer Michael Cronin will be involved in the restoration.

Although those earlier efforts saw varying degrees of success, there is cause for optimism in the Shoals. In 2003, the Staple Singers manager/producer Al Bell said to the *Arkansas Review* that he was

> *now obsessed with the idea of not wanting to die and go to my grave with this knowledge that I have in my head, that I know young people that want to get involved in this business will not be able to read in a book and find there isn't a college or university in this country that can teach them. You have to live it and really have to be born and operating in the business during the period of time that I was born and operating in the business. I want to share that with as many people as possible so that it's out of my head and in some other people's heads so they can take advantage of it and not die and take it to my grave with me. Alive today, there may be one or two people that know what I know about this business. And that bothers me.*

Perhaps Bell's dream is coming true.

19

ONWARD

"Muscle Shoals" is seeing a resurgence. It's because of John Paul White's Single Lock Records. It's because of that garage behind Pegasus Records and Tapes where bands now have a place to play. It's because of Belle Adair and The Bear and Doc Dailey and the Magnolia Devil and those before them like Jason Isbell and the 400 Unit and the Secret Sisters. This place is special again. It just took some folks moving away and coming back, revisiting what they had all along in a new context and swelling with pride.
—music writer and Rogersville native Blake Ells in a column on music blog
Birmingham Box Set

Although there haven't been any hits produced in Muscle Shoals Sound since the Black Keys' rapid departure, the area's musical lineage continues. In recent years, the area's musicians have often been lauded at the American Music Association's annual awards. "Members of the Shoals music community say this kind of publicity can only be helpful for Shoals acts looking for a big break or at least a chance to get their music in front of a larger audience," the *TimesDaily*'s Russ Corey wrote in a 2013 article. "I think any extra light shown on Muscle Shoals is a good thing," songwriter Mike Pyle said to Corey.

Alabama Music Hall of Fame curator Dick Cooper estimates the area now houses seventy active studios; Cooper has one of his own, although he has only recorded a few albums there. Swamper Jimmy Johnson is among that number, as well, and has recently returned to vintage analog equipment

As drivers today cross into Muscle Shoals on Alabama Highway 17, they're greeted by a sign boasting the area's musical reputation. *Author's collection.*

after years of utilizing digital technology. Cooper said nearly everyone he knows in the local music business has a studio of some sort.

Patterson Hood, son of Swamper David Hood, grew up around the studio and went on to found Athens, Georgia–based band Drive-By Truckers with nearby Tuscumbia native Mike Cooley in 1996.

"I grew up fiercely proud of my hometown and my father and the beautiful music they made," Hood wrote in an essay for the web publication *Bitter Southerner.* "Unfortunately, my coming of age coincided with the Muscle Shoals R&B scene ending, or at least losing its worldwide relevance."

The quiet of downtown Sheffield, Alabama, belies the music industry that thrives nearby. *George F. Landegger Collection of Alabama Photographs in Carol M. Highsmith's America, Library of Congress, Prints and Photographs Division. Gift, George F. Landegger, 2010 (DLC/PP-2010:090).*

While that may have been so, musicians from the Shoals area are now gaining popularity internationally—and that includes Hood himself.

"These acts all found a musical home in the Shoals, but they mostly hailed from elsewhere; the town and its studio space were more traveler's rest than homestead—until now," Rachael Maddux wrote in *Southern Living* in January 2013.

The band has seen a handful of members rotate through in its eighteen-year history, among them fellow Shoals native Jason Isbell. A son of Green Hill, Alabama, Isbell became one of the band's dominant songwriters during his six-year tenure with DBT. Favorites such as "Never Gonna Change" pay homage to the area with lines like "You can throw me in the Colbert County jailhouse / You can throw me off the Wilson Dam / But there ain't much difference in the man I wanna be and the man I really am."

Isbell left DBT in 2007, around the time of his divorce from the band's then bassist Shonna Tucker. In the years since, he has spread the Shoals influence as a solo artist and the lead of Jason Isbell and the 400 Unit. The name itself is another callback to the area that birthed this music; the 400 Unit is the nickname for the psych ward at Florence's Eliza Coffee Memorial Hospital. Isbell has recorded at FAME, and his affection for his home state is clear in songs such as "Alabama Pines." In the song's plaintive lyrics, Isbell cries out for home. The album title, *Here We Rest*, is also a reflection of the state in which he was reared, as it was Alabama's original motto.

How the Swampers Changed American Music

When I was writing these songs, I tried to keep the focus on that kind of music found in Muscle Shoals.
—former Drive-By Trucker and Green Hill native Jason Isbell to the Arizona Daily Star *on his debut solo album* Sirens of the Ditch

He carries a torch for the Muscle Shoals sound. In a review of Isbell's 2007 album, *Sirens of the Ditch, Esquire* magazine wrote, "What might just be the best soul record you'll buy this year also offers something grander: 11 new reasons to be thankful for the legacy of Muscle Shoals."

But Muscle Shoals never ceased to birth influential musicians; many have ascended to regional, national and international renown in recent years. John Paul White was among the first in this recent wave. Although he had long worked as a musician and a songwriter, White captured lightning in a bottle when he teamed up with former contemporary Christian artist Joy Williams. The duo met during a songwriting session in Nashville, and the creative chemistry was palpable.

The duo's first headlining show, at Birmingham's WorkPlay Theatre in 2010, sold out. Although White and Williams hadn't yet released an album, the crowd had clearly made itself familiar with their music. Local adult album alternative radio station Live 100.5, renowned as a tastemaker, had the group in heavy rotation, and a free download of a show from Decatur, Georgia's Eddie's Attic must have made an impression.

Any time you walked into a club or saw a show, you'd end up seeing somebody who played on a record you grew up loving. You knew that was the kind of musician you had to become to play around here.
—musician John Paul White of the Civil Wars and Single Lock Records to Southern Living

The band went on to release *Barton Hollow,* which achieved gold-record status and won two Grammy Awards, and followed up with *The Civil Wars,* which included the Grammy-winning song "From This Valley." White and Williams went their separate ways in late 2012. Although the Civil Wars' moment in the limelight has passed, White remains influential. In 2013, he teamed up with fellow musician Ben Tanner and financial advisor Will Trapp to form Florence-based Single Lock Records. The label's name references the Wilson Dam, and its existence is an appropriate nod to the area's history.

"The musical history of [North Alabama] has everything to do with the recording studio and very little to do with live playing," Tanner said to

American Songwriter magazine. "Back in the real heyday, in the '60s and '70s, none of those players were really interested in having a live venue."

Part of the past challenge for live venues was being located in a dry county, explained FAME's Rodney Hall. But now entrepreneurs like Tanner are giving it another go; Single Lock Records in 2013 teamed up with designer Billy Reid to open music venue 116 Mobile. And although they are now partners in a number of business ventures, White's influence on Tanner has been marked in other ways.

Some say the Civil Wars' success opened the door for another 'Bama-bred band. Alabama Shakes formed in Athens, Alabama, just forty-seven miles southeast of the Shoals, when most of the band members were still in high school. Tanner is the band's keyboard player.

The band paid its dues the traditional way, performing shows at bars near the University of Alabama and around the state—much as members of the Muscle Shoals Rhythm Section had done decades earlier. The band quickly became an NPR darling. (It might not have hurt that NPR Music's Ann Powers resides in Tuscaloosa, Alabama.)

Even before the band's debut, *Boys and Girls*, was on record store shelves, the band drew attention to itself with performances on *Conan* and a successful national tour. Before long, it was on best-of lists throughout popular media.

I knew it [Muscle Shoals] *was there, and I knew something really important happened there musically. It just took growing up to start digging and realize what did go on.*
—*Alabama Shakes' Heath Fogg to* Southern Living

The band's success was great enough to earn another fledgling Alabama band the label "the next Alabama Shakes," at least among local music fans. St. Paul and the Broken Bones formed in Birmingham in August 2012, and within months, guitarist and Muscle Shoals native Browan Lollar spoke to media more enthusiastically about that effort than his solo work.

Although young, Lollar had experience from which to speak as a founding member of Isbell's 400 Unit. And sure enough, St. Paul and the Broken Bones' *Half the City*, released by Single Lock Records, was a 2014 Americana Music Association nominee for emerging act of the year.

The Shoals' influence continues with each passing year, and the 2010s have been something of a sweet spot for musicians in the region.

A vintage postcard sends greetings from the Shoals area. The majority of the images highlight the TVA's Wilson Dam. *Anderson News Company, Florence, Alabama.*

> *"Where we come from, a lot of people can sing like this," Lydia said.*
> *"L.A. people are always asking us, 'Where did you learn to sing?'" Laura said.*
> *"'[Was it] voice lessons?'"*
> *"No, we just went to church every Sunday."*
> —*The Secret Sisters' Laura and Lydia Rogers to the* TimesDaily

The Secret Sisters, caramel-voiced sisters who have toured with such acts as Ray LaMontagne and Nickel Creek, also hail from the Shoals. "I just wanted to get out. When I was 18, I wanted to live in a tiny, expensive apartment in the big city. I wanted to be an It girl," the Secret Sisters' Laura Rogers said to the *Sunday Times.* "Now, that's the last thing in the world I care about."

The girls' allegiance to their home became clearer still after parts of north and central Alabama were wrecked by tornadoes in April 2011. The sisters were on tour in Australia, and although their family was safe, the Rogers sisters' hearts remained in Alabama. As writer Rachael Maddux explained in *Southern Living,* "Laura and Lydia felt heartbroken and helpless, so they coped the best way they knew: they wrote a song. 'Tomorrow Will Be Kinder' is a gently sorrowful, hymn-like elegy, and it found an unexpected second life on the movie soundtrack for the first installment of the wildly popular Hunger Games series."

The story about what happened in Muscle Shoals in the 1960s and 1980s could fill a whole bookcase. What happened in Muscle Shoals was recognized by the music industry at that time as a key element in American music. We're looking at how everything converged to form the perfect situation, the perfect opportunity. The opposite of the perfect storm. It was something that had never been seen before and hasn't been seen since.

—*In the Family Productions owner Wallace Sears to the* TimesDaily *(Sears is working on a documentary,* Sweet Home Alabama—The Music of Muscle Shoals*)*

Zion Godchaux, son of FAME and Muscle Shoals Sound singer and Grateful Dead member Donna Jean Godchaux-MacKay, is now making music as part of the electronic band BoomBox. Although the band avoids genre labels, it's clear that the area's rock, blues and soul history have influenced the musicians. Likewise, roots music and rock-and-roll influenced bands the Bear, Belle Adair, Doc Dailey and Magnolia Devil, Dylan LeBlanc and numerous other local bands are beginning to make waves across the region and beyond. And these are certainly not the only bands with Shoals ties that are currently making noise. As a new generation of musicians pours both out of and into Muscle Shoals, the beat will go on.

BIBLIOGRAPHY

BOOKS

Appleford, Steve. *The Rolling Stones: Rip this Joint; The Stories Behind Every Song.* Boston: Da Capo Press, 2001.

Bowman, Rob. *Soulsville U.S.A: The Story of Stax Records.* New York: Schirmer Trade Books, 1997.

Fuqua, Christopher S. *Music Fell on Alabama.* Birmingham, AL: Crane Hill Publishers, 1991.

Guralnik, Peter. *Sweet Soul Music: Rhythm and Blues and the Southern Dream of Freedom.* Boston: Little, Brown and Company, 1986.

Janovitz, Bill. *Rocks Off: 50 Tracks That Tell the Story of the Rolling Stones.* New York: St. Martin's Press, 2013.

Komar, Edward, ed. *Encyclopedia of the Blues.* Vol. 1, *A–J.* New York: Routledge, 2006.

Morthland, John. *The Best of Country Music.* New York: Doubleday, 1984.

Wexler, Jerry, and David Ritz. *Rhythm and the Blues: A Life in American Music.* New York: Alfred A. Knopf, 1993.

Whitburn, Joel. *The* Billboard *Book of Top 40 Hits.* New York: Billboard Books, 1992.

Younger, Richard. *Get a Shot of Rhythm & Blues: The Arthur Alexander Story.* Tuscaloosa: University of Alabama Press, 2000.

BIBLIOGRAPHY

INTERVIEWS

Bak, Bonnie (public relations, Muscle Shoals Music Foundation). Telephone interview with the author, May 20, 2014.

Cooper, Dick (journalist, photographer, Alabama Music Hall of Fame curator and former Muscle Shoals Sound employee). In-person interview with the author, April 10, 2014.

Hall, Rodney (Muscle Shoals Music Foundation board chairman, president of FAME Studios, son of Rick Hall). Telephone interview with the author, May 23, 2014.

Johnson, Jimmy (Muscle Shoals Rhythm Section member and Muscle Shoals Sound Studio owner). In-person interview with the author, April 10, 2014.

Webster, Noel (former owner, Muscle Shoals Sound Studio). In-person interview with the author, August 11, 2013.

———. Telephone interview with the author, February 10, 2014.

MAGAZINES AND NEWSPAPERS

Associated Press. "Beats Electronics Backing Muscle Shoals Upgrades." *Billboard*, November 26, 2013.

———. "Historic Music Studio in Muscle Shoals Closes." February 25, 2005.

Bates, Bob. "As Recording Fame Grows, Show Biggies Beat Path to Muscle Shoals." *Birmingham (AL) News*, February 3, 1971.

Beals, Jonas. "Southern Rockers' Live Show Still a Wild Ride, Even with Female Influence Drive-By Truckers Are True to 'Bama Roots." *(Fredericksburg, VA) Free Lance-Star*, May 8, 2008.

Berry, Lucy. "Foundation Buys the Original Muscle Shoals Sound Studios." *Huntsville Times*, June 23, 2013.

———. "Foundation Purchases the Original Muscle Shoals Sound Studios, Which Recorded Rolling Stones, Bob Dylan and More." AL.com, June 20, 2013.

———. "Group Raising Funds to Buy Iconic Muscle Shoals Sound Studios." *Huntsville Times*, June 9, 2013.

———. "Walk through Legendary Muscle Shoals Sound Studios before Dr. Dre's Beats Electronics Revives Historic Building." AL.com, March 26, 2014.

Billboard. "*Billboard*'s Top Album Picks." March 4, 1974

———. "'Take a Letter, Maria' Singer R.B. Greaves Dies at 68." October 3, 2012.

Birmingham News. "Again the Question of 'Muscle' or 'Mussel' Shoals." October 4, 1934.

———. "Sound at the Shoals." March 9, 1971.

Brantley, Mike. "Made in Alabama." *Mobile Register,* May 22, 2005.

Brown, Mick. "Deep Soul: How Muscle Shoals Became Music's Most Unlikely Hit Factory." *(London) Telegraph,* March 7, 2014.

Bumgardner, Ed. "A New Team of Truckers on the Road, Eager to Rock 'n' Roll." *Winston-Salem (NC) Journal,* October 30, 2008.

Busdeker, Jon. "25 Best Songs by Alabama Artists." *Huntsville Times,* May 16, 2010.

Carlson, Sarah, "There Never Were Such Devoted Sisters." *(Florence) TimesDaily,* October 8, 2010.

Carlton, Bob. "Billy Bob Thornton Talks Film, Music, Mayberry, Muscle Shoals Sound Inspired Movie Star." *Birmingham News,* March 8, 2008.

———. "Sounds of the Shoals: A Magical, Musical Mystery Tour." *Birmingham News,* March 28, 1999.

Cave, Damien, Matt Diehl, Gavin Edwards, Jenny Eliscu, David Fricke, Lauren Gitlin, Matt Hendrickson, Kirk Miller, Austin Scaggs and Rob Sheffield. "Two Hours Remake Soul." *Rolling Stone,* June 24, 2004.

Clark, Shelton. "He'll Take You There: David Hood's Legacy as the Muscle of Muscle Shoals." *Bass Player,* June 2013.

Cochran, Debi. "Songwriters: Hit-makers Grab a Share of the Spotlight." *Decatur Daily,* November 28, 1982.

Collins, Lisa. "In the Spirit." *Billboard,* July 6, 1996.

Colurso, Mary. "Alabama's Jason Isbell, St. Paul & Broken Bones among Nominees for 2014 Americana Music Awards." AL.com, May 12, 2014.

———. "Muscle Shoals Magic Parnell Returns to Legendary Studio with Winning Results." *Birmingham News,* July 13, 2001.

———. "Music Highways Travel Down Memory Lane to Hit Alabama High Notes." *Birmingham News,* March 19, 2004.

———. "The Music Quits Playing at Muscle Shoals Sound Studios." *Birmingham News,* February 25, 2005.

———. "Year of Alabama Music People You Should Know." *Birmingham News,* March 4, 2011.

———. "Year of Alabama Music People You Should Know." *Birmingham News,* March 25, 2011.

————. "Year of Alabama Music People You Should Know: Muscle Shoals Rhythm Section." *Birmingham News*, December 9, 2011.

————. "Year of Alabama Music People You Should Know: Percy Sledge." *Birmingham News*, May 27, 2011.

Corey, Russ. "The Beat Goes On." *(Florence, AL) TimesDaily*, November 27, 2013.

————. "Dark Days for Hall of Fame." *(Florence, AL) TimesDaily*, January 19, 2013.

————. "Documentary 'Humbles' Shoals Music Community." *(Florence, AL) TimesDaily*, February 28, 2013.

————. "Foundation Acquires Sound Studio 3614 Jackson Highway." *(Florence, AL) TimesDaily*, June 20, 2013.

————. "Hall of Fame Attracting Visitors Again." *(Florence, AL) TimesDaily*, December 17, 2013.

————. "Hall of Fame Frustration." *(Florence, AL) TimesDaily*, February 3, 2013.

————. "Historical Note: Tiny Studio Receives Recognition for Huge Past." *(Florence, AL) TimesDaily*, November 13, 2005.

————. "Movie Aided Hall's Revival." *(Florence, AL) TimesDaily*, September 28, 2013.

————. "'Muscle Shoals' Draws Praise." *(Florence, AL) TimesDaily*, December 30, 2013.

————. "Muscle Shoals Foundation to Buy 3614 Jackson Highway." *(Florence, AL) TimesDaily*, May 11, 2013.

————. "Music Hall of Fame Could Be Moving." *(Florence, AL) TimesDaily*, April 10, 2013.

————. "Part 1: Museum Houses a Treasure of Music Memorabilia." *(Florence, AL) TimesDaily*, August 25, 2013.

————. "Part 2: Seeking a Solution for Alabama Music Hall of Fame." *(Florence, AL) TimesDaily*, August 26, 2013.

————. "Proceeds from Premiere Go to Foundation, Hall of Fame Exhibit." *(Florence, AL) TimesDaily*, February 26, 2013.

————. "Recent Success of Shoals Bands Aids Rising Artists." *(Florence, AL) TimesDaily*, January 23, 2013.

————. "2nd Film on Shoals Music in the Works." *(Florence, AL) TimesDaily*, March 23, 2013.

————. "Shoals Museum's Cost Justified by Attraction of Visitors." *TimesDaily*. Reprinted, *Huntsville Times*, October 20, 2008.

————. "Some Say Museum Needs High-Tech Features." *(Florence, AL) TimesDaily*, August 26, 2013.

———. "Talk of the Town: Raves for 'Muscle Shoals' Documentary." *(Florence, AL) TimesDaily*, January 27, 2013.

———. "Tourism Music to Ears of Shoals." *(Florence, AL) TimesDaily*, April 14, 2013.

Corey, Russ, and Mike Goens, "Legacy in Peril." *(Florence, AL) TimesDaily*, August 25, 2013.

Crandall, Bill, Gavin Edwards, Jenny Eliscu, et al. "500 Greatest Songs of All Time." *Rolling Stone*, December 9, 2004.

Crisler, Daniel E. "From Studios to Streets: 'The Shoals' Sound Can Still Be Heard—Just in a Different Key." *Get Set Mag*, March 2013.

Cromer, Ben. "Beckett's Journey from Muscle Shoals to Nashville Ends with Country Success." *Billboard*, May 28, 1994.

Cubarrubia, RJ. "George Jackson, 'Old Time Rock & Roll' Writer, Dead at 68." *Rolling Stone*, April 15, 2013.

Danborn, Joe. "The Crash of Lynyrd Skynyrd." *Mobile Register*, October 23, 2002.

DeLuca, Dan. "In 'Muscle Shoals,' the Music Is Color-Blind." *Philadelphia Inquirer*, October 11, 2013.

Detroit News. "The Golden Age of the Motown Sound." February 29, 2000.

Edwards, Jennifer. "Forum Looks at Racial Harmony of Musicians." *(Florence, AL) TimesDaily*, October 12, 2013.

Flippo, Chet. "Matthew, Mark, Luke and Willie." *Texas Monthly*, September 1975.

———. "*Phases and Stages* Willie Nelson." Review. *Rolling Stone*, March 14, 1974.

(Florence, AL) TimesDaily. "Alabama Music Hall of Fame Board of Directors." August 25, 2013.

———. "Alabama Music Hall of Fame Timeline." August 25, 2013.

———. "Funding for Hall of Fame." Editorial. January 30, 2013.

———. "State Funding for the Alabama Music Hall of Fame." August 25, 2013.

Fricke, David. "*Brothers* the Black Keys." Review. *Rolling Stone*, May 17, 2010.

———. "Pickett's Most Wicked." *Rolling Stone*, February 9, 2006.

Gay, Gerald M. "Former Trucker Brings Solo Act to Congress." *(Tucson) Arizona Daily Star*, August 2, 2007.

Gordon, Tom. "Will Rock Music Turn to 'More Basic Bop'?" *Anniston Star*, March 6, 1975.

Herald, Florence, letter to the editor. "Spell It 'Muscle.'" *Birmingham News*, October 12, 1934.

BIBLIOGRAPHY

Hoard, Christian. "The Black Keys' Muscle Shoals Odyssey." *Rolling Stone*, December 10, 2009.

Holden, Stephen. *"There Goes Rhymin' Simon* Paul Simon." Review. *Rolling Stone*, June 21, 1973.

Howard, Jennifer Crossley. "Alabama Museum, in Area Where Stars Found Sound, Seeks an Audience: Tourists." *New York Times*, October 7, 2013.

Hubbard, Perri. "'Muscle Shoals' Heart and Soul of a Musical Movement." *Get Set Mag*, March 2013.

Hume, Janice. "MSMA Takes Stand for Music Industry." *(Florence, AL) TimesDaily*, April 11, 1982.

———. "Public Television Special Will Feature History of Alabama Music Industry." *Mobile Press-Register*, November 14, 1982.

Huntsville Times. "Alabama Music Hall of Fame Inductees." January 29, 1993.

———. "Five Muscle Shoals Sound Songs." November 9, 1997.

Inman, Davis. "Alabama Sounds: The Story of Muscle Shoals." *American Songwriter*, March 2012.

Itzkoff, Dave. "Seen Much Better Days: Rolling Stones Return to 'Main Street.'" *New York Times*, February 26, 2010.

Johnson, Francie. "A Musical Road: Muscle Shoals' Rich Heritage in Music Makes Its Way to Tuscaloosa." *Crimson White*, November 4, 2013.

Kleiner, Dick, and Newspaper Enterprise Association. "Post-Oscar Reflections and Poop." *(Fort Walton Beach, FL) Playground Daily News*, April 21, 1970.

Koch, Stephen. "Al Bell Takes Us There: An Interview." *Arkansas Review: A Journal of Delta Studies* 32, no. 1 (2001).

Landau, Jon. *"Sticky Fingers* Rolling Stones." Review. *Rolling Stone*, April 23, 1971.

Langer, Andy. "The Muscle Shoals Sound: Man at His Best (Featuring Jason Isbell)." *Esquire*, July 2007.

Liberty, John. "'Bama's BoomBox to Bring 'Funky, Sweaty Dance Party,'" *Kalamazoo (MI) Gazette*, November 1, 2007.

Loder, Kurt. *"Saved* Bob Dylan." Review. *Rolling Stone*, September 18, 1980.

(London) Times. "Jerry Wexler: Pioneering Music Producer Who Produced Aretha Franklin." August 18, 2008.

Maddux, Rachael. "The New Sound of Muscle Shoals." *Southern Living*, January 2013.

Marcus, Griel. *"Let It Bleed* Rolling Stones." Review. *Rolling Stone*, December 27, 1969.

Marsh, Dave. *"Breakaway* Art Garfunkel." Review. *Rolling Stone*, December 4, 1975.

————. "Lynyrd Skynyrd Album to Be Released." *Rolling Stone*. Reprinted in *Sun-Telegram*, May 23, 1978.

————. "*Skynyrd's First and...Last* Lynyrd Skynyrd." Review. *Rolling Stone*, November 16, 1978.

Mobile Register. "Senator Should Sing a New Song on Museum." Editorial. February 25, 2006.

Nelson, Paul. "*Atlantic Crossing* Rod Stewart." Review. *Rolling Stone*, September 25, 1975.

Oden, Demps. A., letter to the editor. "'Muscle' or 'Mussel' Shoals." *Birmingham News*, October 12, 1934.

Pace, Terry. "Lynyrd Skynyrd Rock Band Returns to 'Sweet Home.'" *Huntsville Times*, March 23, 1997.

Palmer, David. "Lennon and That Shoals Music Magic." *(Florence, AL) TimesDaily*, November 16, 1984.

Palmer, Robert. "Famous Sound." *(Florence, AL) TimesDaily*, December 31, 2013.

————. "Heard around the World: Muscle Shoals Sound Is Seen as the Embodiment of 'Treasure and Terrible Beauty.'" *(Florence, AL) TimesDaily*, March 11, 2001.

————. "Spreading the Word Far, Wide." *(Florence, AL) TimesDaily*, March 2013.

————. "Thrilling Sounds: Project Revives Famous Studio." *(Florence, AL) TimesDaily*, May 8, 2001.

Patterson, Rob, and Pop Scene Service. "Delbert McClinton Has a Hit after 25 Years." *Salina (Kansas) Journal Sunflower*, March 8, 1981.

Paul, Alan. "Prime Cuts: Lynyrd Skynyrd." *Guitar World*, March 4, 2009.

Peisner, David. "Muscle Shoals Revival: Alabama Shakes Takes Off." *Rolling Stone*, February 2, 2012.

Perrone, Pierre. "Barry Beckett: Musician Who Helped Form the Muscle Shoals Rhythm Section." *Independent*, August 19, 2009.

P.G. "The Sounds of Soul City." *Billboard*, February 9, 2013.

Poet, J. "The Black Keys." *Soma Magazine*, July 2010.

Potton, Ed. "Sacred Spaces Are Dying Out." *(London) Times*, August 21, 2012.

Purcell, Andrew. "The Black Keys—'It's Ridiculous to Say That We Play the Blues.'" *(London) Independent*, July 9, 2010.

Puterbaugh, Parke. "Muscle Shoals for Sale." *Rolling Stone*, August 21, 2003.

Rachlis, Kit. "*Night Moves* Bob Seger." Review. *Rolling Stone*, January 13, 1977.

Rassenfoss, Joe. "Muscle Shoals Residents in Tune with Studios Now." *Birmingham Post-Herald*, May 16, 1980.

Rawls, Phillip. "Singing Senator Seeks to Save Alabama Music Hall of Fame." Associated Press. Reprinted in *Birmingham News*, February 23, 2006.

Richman, Simmy. "How We Met: Joy Williams & John Paul White." *(London) Independent*, March 18, 2012.

Ryan, Shawn. "A Matter of Black & White. R&B Singers Mixed with Country/Gospel Backup to Produce That Special Shoals Sound." *Huntsville Times*, January 21, 1994.

Simons, Dave. "Mark Neill: Recording the Black Keys at Muscle Shoals." *Sound on Sound*, August 2011.

———. "Tales from the Top: The Rolling Stones' *Sticky Fingers* (1971)." *BMI*, January 30, 2009.

Sinclair, David. "Never Such Devoted Sisters." *Sunday Times*, May 1, 2011.

Sing Out! "Muscle Shoals Sound Studios." Summer 2005.

Smallwood, Dean. "Rock 'n' Shoals." *Huntsville Times*, November 9, 1997.

Sparks, Rayburn. "Records, Hit Records Made in Muscle Shoals." Associated Press. Reprinted in *Anniston Star*, May 30, 1971.

Specker, Lawrence. "Muscle Shoals." *(Mobile) Press Register*, March 2, 2001.

Stephens, Glenn. "Look Out Nashville, Muscle Shoals Is Here." United Press International, March 6, 1977.

Swartz, Captain George W., letter to the editor. "Muscle Not Mussel." *Huntsville Times*, February 25, 1931.

Talbott, Chris. "Firm to Back Muscle Shoals Studio Upgrades." Associated Press, November 26, 2013.

Tennille, Andy. "Muscle Men: A Look at the Magicians Who Conjured the Muscle Shoals Sound." *Harp* (September/October 2005).

Thomas, Tom. "Tom Thomas' Turntable." *(Troy, NY) Record Newspapers*, June 12, 1971.

Van Syckle, Katie. "Sundance Doc 'Muscle Shoals' Features Bono, Aretha, Rolling Stones." *Rolling Stone*, January 24, 2013.

Waddell, Ray. "I Like That Banjo and I Like Balls-to-the-Wall Rock." *Billboard*, May 1, 2004.

Wake, Matt. "Finding Music Inspiration in Muscle Shoals." *Huntsville Times*, September 20, 2012.

———. "'Muscle Shoals' Director Greg 'Freddy' Camalier on His Documentary Film Chronicling North Alabama's Musical Magic." AL.com, February 21, 2013.

Wallen, Paul. "For Father, Son It'll Be Night in the Hood." *Huntsville Times*, April 26, 2012.

Walsh, Christopher. "The Music Ends Famed Muscle Shoals Studio Folds." *Billboard*, March 5, 2005.

Weber, Bruce. "Jerry Wexler, a Behind-the-Scenes Force in Black Music, Is Dead at 91." *New York Times*, August 15, 2008.

Wenner, Jann S. "*Slow Train Coming* Bob Dylan." Review. *Rolling Stone*, September 20, 1979.

Wessel, John. "Hall of Fame Is Special for Wexler." *Huntsville Times*, January 27, 1993.

———. "Muscle Shoals Heritage Is Music and More Music." *Huntsville Times*, December 14, 1999.

Whitley, Carla Jean. "Shaking It Up: The Boys and Girl of Athens' Alabama Shakes Have the Music Scene Talking," *Birmingham* magazine, April 2012.

Whitty, Stephen. "'Muscle Shoals': The Real Sweet Home Alabama." *(Newark, NJ) Star-Ledger*, October 4, 2013.

Zagier, Alan Scher. "Blues Museum to Call St. Louis Home, Sweet Home." Associated Press, October 20, 2013.

MUSIC

Alexander, Arthur. *You Better Move On.* MCA, 1993, compact disc. Originally released in 1961.

The Black Keys. *Brothers.* Nonesuch, 2010, compact disc.

Bob Seger and the Silver Bullet Band. *Night Moves.* Capitol, 1999, compact disc. Originally released in 1976.

———. *Stranger in Town.* Capitol, 2001, compact disc. Originally released in 1978.

Cher. *3614 Jackson Highway.* Rhino, 2013, compact disc. Originally released in 1969.

Dylan, Bob. *Slow Train Coming.* Sony, 2004, compact disc. Originally released in 1979.

Franklin, Aretha. *I Never Loved a Man (The Way I Love You).* Atlantic, 1995, compact disc. Originally released in 1967.

Greaves, R.B. *R.B. Greaves.* Collectables, 2002, compact disc. Originally released in 1969.

Lynyrd Skynyrd. *Second Helping.* MCA, 1997, compact disc. Originally released in 1974.

———. *Skynyrd's First: The Complete Muscle Shoals Album.* MCA, 1998, compact disc. Originally released in 1978 as *Skynyrd's First and...Last.*

Rolling Stones. *Sticky Fingers.* Universal Music Enterprises, 2009, compact disc. Originally released in 1971.

Simon, Paul. *There Goes Rhymin' Simon.* Sony Legacy, 2011, compact disc. Originally released in 1973.

The Staple Singers. *Be Altitude: Respect Yourself.* Concord Music, 2011, compact disc. Originally released in 1972.

Stewart, Rod. *Atlantic Crossing.* Rhino, 2011, compact disc. Originally released in 1975.

WEBSITES AND BLOGS

Alabama Alcoholic Beverage Control Board. http://www.abcboard.state.al.us (accessed March 24, 2014).

"All the Number One Albums: 1969." *Official Charts Company.* http://www.officialcharts.com/all-the-number-one-albums-list/_/1969/.

Billboard. "The Hot 100—1966 Archive." http://www.billboard.com/archive/charts/1966/hot-100 (accessed March 22, 2014).

"Bobby Denton." http://bobbydenton.com.

Borgerson, Bruce. "Glory Days: Muscle Shoals 1967–1972, 1972–1980." PrsoundWeb.com, 2004. http://www.prosoundweb.com/article/the_glory_days_of_muscle_shoals (accessed May 12, 2014).

The City of Florence, Alabama. www.florenceal.org (retrieved May 5, 2014).

Deming, Mark. "3614 Jackson Highway." Review. Allmusic.com. http://www.allmusic.com/album/3614-jackson-highway-mw0000694186.

Ells, Blake. "Exploring the Boundaries of 'Muscle Shoals': A Weekend at the Billy Reid Shindig." Birmingham Box Set (blog), August 26, 2013. http://blog.AL.com/birmingham-box-set/2013/08/post_31.html.

———. "Good People Brewing Company Welcomes Mike Cooley for Camp McDowell Benefit on October 12." Birmingham Box Set (blog), September 24, 2013. http://blog.AL.com/birmingham-box-set/2013/09/post_39.html.

———. "Rock and Roll Hall of Famer Spooner Oldham Relives 'Muscle Shoals.'" Birmingham Box Set (blog), August 22, 2013. http://blog.AL.com/birmingham-box-set/2013/08/post_30.html.

———. "The Swampers Lead a 'Muscle Shoals Review' in Sweet Home Alabama." Birmingham Box Set (blog), October 24, 2013. http://blog.AL.com/birmingham-box-set/2013/10/the_swampers_lead_a_muscle_sho.html.

Fuqua, C.S. "Jerry Wexler, Godfather of Muscle Shoals Music, Remembered." New South Books (blog), August 26, 2008. http://www.newsouthbooks.com/pages/2008/08/26/jerry-wexler-godfather-of-muscle-shoals-music-remembered.

Grammy Awards. "Past Winners Search." grammy.com (accessed May 14, 2014).

"Help Raise Funds to Purchase the Legendary Muscle Shoals Sound Studios 3614 Jackson Highway," http://www.volumebee.com/volume?vid=102202913 (accessed April 23, 2014).

Hood, Patterson. "The New(er) South." Bitter Southerner, http://bittersoutherner.com/patterson-hood-the-newer-south (accessed March 10, 2014).

Lopate, Mitch. "On and Off the Road with Dick Cooper." Swampland, 2000. http://swampland.com/articles/view/title:dick_cooper (accessed April 12, 2014).

"The Malaco Story." malaco.com (accessed May 14, 2014).

"Muscle Shoals Rhythm Section." Alabama Music Hall of Fame. http://www.alamhof.org/inductees/timeline/1995/muscle-shoals-rhythm-section (accessed December 10, 2013).

North Mississippi Allstars. http://www.nmallstars.com/about.

Northwest Alabama Regional Airport Authority. http://www.flytheshoals.com.

O'Hehir, Andrew. "'Muscle Shoals' and the GOP's Quest for Purity." *Salon*, September 28, 2013. http://www.salon.com/2013/09/28/%E2%80%9Cmuscle_shoals%E2%80%9D_and_the_gop%E2%80%99s_quest_for_purity.

Olson, Peter B. "Eddie Hinton." Encyclopedia of Alabama, 2009, accessed May 27, 2014.

116 Mobile Street. http://journal.billyreid.com/post/59604506714/116-mobile-street (retrieved May 24, 2014).

Osato, Kelly S. "The Muscle Shoals Documentary: A Tale of Two Studios, One Sound." *Amoeba*, October 17, 2013. http://www.amoeba.com/blog/2013/10/grow-sound-tree/the-muscle-shoals-documentary-a-tale-of-two-studios-one-sound.html.

"Pete Carr Discography." playthatguitar.com/Discog.html (accessed May 27, 2014).

Rentner, Simon. "Evolution of a Song: 'St. Louis Blues,'" A Blog Supreme (blog, NPR), August 10, 2011. http://www.npr.org/blogs/ablogsupreme/2011/08/10/139377374/evolution-of-a-song-st-louis-blues.

Ruhlmann, William. "Joan Baez Honest Lullaby." Review. All Music, accessed May 27, 2014.

"Single Lock Records." Alabama Chanin (blog), May 28, 2013. http://alabamachanin.com/journal/2013/05/single-lock-records.

Smith, Michael B., and Roxanne Crutcher. "Pete Carr: The Most Important Things in Life are Rock and Roll, and a Hot Carr." Swampland, 2000, accessed May 27, 2014.

"Timeline: The History of Motown." Motown Museum. http://www.motownmuseum.org/motown-sound/timeline/timeline-1972 (accessed May 14, 2014).

"Tom Dowd Biography." Rock and Roll Hall of Fame. http://rockhall.com/inductees/tom-dowd/bio (accessed May 14, 2014).

Wiser, Carl, and Nicholas Tozier, "Aretha to the Black Keys: The Muscle Shoals Story." *Songfacts*, June 16, 2012. http://www.songfacts.com/blog/writing/aretha_to_the_black_keys_the_muscle_shoals_story.

OTHER SOURCES

Beats Electronics. "Beats Electronics Revives the Muscle Shoals Sound Studio." News release, November 26, 2013, PRNewswire.

Bowman, Rob. "Malaco Records: The Last Soul Company." Box set liner notes, March 23, 1999.

Elliot, Debbie. "The Legendary Muscle Shoals Sound: Alabama Studios Rolled Out Big "Hits of '60s and '70s." NPR, September 20, 2003.

"Gold Platinum Database: The Black Keys." Music Canada. musiccanada.com (accessed May 14, 2014).

Gross, Terry. "Jason Isbell Locates His Musical Compass on 'Southeastern.'" *Fresh Air*. NPR, July 17, 2013.

Hansen, Liane. "Tom Dowd: Fluent in 'The Language of Music.'" *Weekend Edition Sunday*. NPR, August 15, 2004.

Jenkins, Mark. "Music Doc Packs 'Muscle' (Plus a Whole Lotta Soul)." NPR, September 26, 2013.

Johnson, D.A. "Company Profile for Malaco Music Group." Press release, August 17, 2012.

Muscle Shoals Chamber of Commerce. "Muscle Shoals District." Brochure, April 30, 1958.

National Register of Historic Places. Muscle Shoals Sound Studio. Sheffield, Colbert County, Alabama, National Register #06000437.

Ochs, Meredith. "Jason Isbell and the 400 Unit: Life Back Home." NPR, April 13, 2011.

Office of Alabama Governor Robert J. Bentley. "Celebrate Muscle Shoals Music Day." News release, October 17, 2003. governor.al.gov.

Thompson, Stephen. "The Civil Wars: A Song of Loyalty, Before It's Tested." NPR, November 7, 2012.

U.S. Congress. Senate. "A Bill to Amend Title 17 of the United States Code to Exempt the Private Noncommercial Recording of Copyrighted Works on Video Recorders from Copyright Infringement." S1758. 97th Congress. *Congressional Record*. congress.gov (accessed May 24, 2014).

Ward, Ed. "A Studio on the Road to 'FAME' for Soul Musicians." NPR, February 3, 2012.

Weekend Edition Saturday. "Profile: Muscle Shoals Sound Studio in Alabama Up for Sale." NPR, September 20, 2003.

FILM

Muscle Shoals. Blu-ray. Directed by Greg "Freddy" Camalier. Magnolia Home Entertainment, 2014.

The Rolling Stones: Gimme Shelter. DVD. Directed by David Maysles, Albert Maysles and Charlotte Zwerin. Maysles Films, 1970.

"SoLost: Midnight Muscle Shoals Music Lesson." *Oxford American* magazine video, 6:03, July 13, 2011. http://www.oxfordamerican.org/articles/2011/jul/13/solost-midnight-muscle-shoals-music-lesson.

INDEX

A

Alexander, Arthur 19, 21, 25
Auerbach, Dan 113, 114, 115, 117,
    118

B

Beckett, Barry 9, 10, 28, 32, 33, 34,
    36, 37, 40, 61, 69, 73, 82, 87,
    92, 103, 104, 122, 127
Birmingham 9, 10, 11, 13, 14, 18,
    28, 32, 33, 39, 40, 46, 47, 56,
    57, 59, 61, 76, 77, 88, 134,
    136, 139
Black Keys, the 56, 111, 113, 114, 116,
    117, 132, 136
Bryant, Paul W. "Bear" 74

C

Carney, Patrick 113, 114, 115, 117, 118
Carter, Clarence 9, 17, 45, 73, 122
Cher 47, 49, 52, 56
Cooper, Dick 36, 37, 56, 59, 77, 122,
    125, 128, 136, 137

D

Denton, Bobby 24, 119, 125, 152
Drive-By Truckers 74, 137
Dylan, Bob 9, 10, 33, 35, 49, 59,
    92–95, 102, 104, 126

F

FAME Recording Studios 11, 17, 24,
    25, 26, 28, 29, 32, 33, 34, 35,
    36, 37, 40, 43, 44, 45, 47, 57,
    78, 97, 119, 122, 127, 131, 133,
    138, 142
Franklin, Aretha 17, 26, 29, 30, 31, 33,
    49, 72, 73, 88, 127

G

Garfunkel, Art 78, 87, 88
Greaves, R.B. 47, 50, 52, 115

H

Hall, Rick 11, 17, 24, 25, 26, 28, 33,
    37, 38, 40, 43, 57, 73, 127
Hall, Rodney 43, 45, 123, 124, 129, 130
Handy, W.C. 16, 18, 56, 57, 122

Hawkins, Roger 10, 28, 30, 32, 34, 37, 40, 69, 73, 78, 87, 104, 127
Hood, David 10, 28, 32, 33, 34, 35, 36, 37, 40, 43, 44, 47, 50, 55, 69, 71, 73, 74, 78, 82, 84, 88, 127, 137
Hood, Patterson 55, 74, 137, 138

I

Iovine, Jimmy 130, 131, 132

J

Jacksonville, Florida 63, 66, 77, 122
Johnson, Dexter 21
Johnson, Jimmy 10, 21, 24, 28, 32, 34, 36, 40, 43, 44, 49, 53, 54, 56, 59, 66, 73, 76, 82, 104, 110, 127, 128, 135, 136

L

Lair, George 25, 43, 124
Lennon, Julian 95, 99, 111
Lynyrd Skynyrd 10, 15, 61, 62, 63, 66, 73, 74

M

Muscle Shoals Music Foundation 111, 127, 129, 130, 133

N

Neill, Mark 113, 114, 115, 116, 117

O

Oldham, Spooner 28, 32, 41, 122, 127

P

Penn, Dan 28, 32, 122, 127
Phillips, Sam 18, 117, 122, 134
Pickett, Wilson 17, 27, 28, 29, 59, 73

R

Rolling Stones 10, 54, 55, 93

S

Seger, Bob 17, 76, 78, 89, 90
Simon, Paul 10, 17, 78, 82, 84, 85, 88
Sledge, Percy 17, 24, 26, 27
Spar Music Company 24, 25, 26
Staple Singers, the 10, 16, 67, 68, 69, 135
Staples, Mavis 70, 71
St. Augustine, Florida 39
Stewart, Rod 24, 78, 88, 89
"Sweet Home Alabama" 10, 15, 66, 73, 142

T

Tune Records 21, 24

U

University of Alabama 18, 32, 45, 73, 140

V

Van Zant, Ronnie 63, 64, 66

W

Webster, Noel 43, 108, 109, 110, 111, 112, 115, 116, 119, 130, 134
Wexler, Jerry 27, 28, 29, 31, 33, 36, 41, 44, 47, 49, 50, 52, 54, 72, 73, 85, 86, 92, 95, 96, 97, 110, 122

ABOUT THE AUTHOR

Carla Jean Whitley is a writer, editor and teacher based in Birmingham, Alabama, where she is managing editor of *Birmingham* magazine. Carla Jean founded the music blog Birmingham Box Set and has also written for *BookPage*, *Paste*, the *Birmingham News*, *Sky* and a variety of other magazines and newspapers. Carla Jean volunteers with literacy organizations and teaches journalism at the University of Alabama and Samford University. Her favorite yoga pose is bakasana, and her favorite cats are orange. This is her first book. Connect with her at carlajeanwhitley.com.